BLACK THEATER IN AMERICA

ALSO BY JAMES HASKINS

The Creoles of Color of New Orleans

The Quiet Revolution:
The Struggle for the Rights of Disabled Americans

BLACK THEATER IN AMERICA

James Haskins

ILLUSTRATED WITH PHOTOGRAPHS

Thomas Y. Crowell   New York

*I am grateful to Laurel Burns and J. M. Stifle
and especially to Kathy Benson for their help.*

Library of Congress Cataloging in Publication Data
Haskins, James, 1941–
Black theater in America.
Bibliography: p.
Includes index.
1. Afro-American theater–History–Juvenile litera-
ture. I. Title.
PN2226.H37 1982   792'.0973   81-43874
ISBN 0-690-04128-4   AACR2
ISBN 0-690-04129-2 (lib. bdg.)

1 2 3 4 5 6 7 8 9 10
FIRST EDITION

Contents

BLACK THEATER
IN AMERICA

1
"To Be or Not to Be"

The Pre-Civil War Theater

On December 21, 1751, *Othello* opened at the Nassau Street Theatre in New York City. It was the first time this play by William Shakespeare had been presented in the American colonies, although it had been performed many times in England. One of Shakespeare's most famous plays, it shows how love can be destroyed by jealousy. A black man named Othello becomes so suspicious of his white wife, Desdemona, that he kills her. Today, the part of Othello is usually played by a black actor. Back in New York City in 1751 it would have been unheard of for a black to appear on a stage in any role. In that performance at the Nassau Street Theatre over 200 years ago the part of Othello was played by a white man.

The actor, Robert Upton, blackened his face, probably with burnt cork, so he would look dark-complected. Everyone knew he was white, but audiences did not demand that a black man play a black part. William Shakespeare had no more expected that a black man would play Othello than he had thought Desdemona would be played by a woman. In Shakespeare's time all female roles were given to boys or young men. Women did not appear on stage in those days.

By the 1750s women were beginning to play the female roles in some plays, but it would be a long time before blacks would be played by blacks. It would be 70 years or so before blacks would have their own theater, and about 100 years before blacks would be allowed on the stages of white theaters. And it would be over 150 years before a real black Othello could play opposite a real white female Desdemona without being run out of town by an angry white audience. This is the story of how these and many other things came to pass, an account of the more than 200-year-old history of black theater in America.

If you have ever been to a school play, you know what theater is. Someone makes up a story, which is then acted out before an audience. If costumes, makeup, and scenery are used, the production will cost money. In the case of school plays, the school usually supplies the necessary funds. If you and your friends are staging the play at home, parents will usually pitch in and supply what's needed. When groups of adults get together and decide to put on a play, they need money too. Sometimes they get donations from businessmen in the community in order to pay for costumes and scenery. Sometimes they charge admission to their performances to help cover expenses. No one involved in such productions expects to earn any money from them.

So far, we have been talking about amateur theater, but in this book we will be talking mostly about professional theater, where plays are put on for profit. To make money in the theater, there must be enough people who want to see plays and those people must have enough money to be able to buy tickets. These conditions were apparently not met in the early days of the American colonies. Although New York was founded in the 1620s (as New Netherland), there is not a single mention of plays or actors there until 1699. Furthermore, no one has ever found a record of a theater of any kind in New York until the 1730s, over a hundred years after New Netherland's founding.

The first theatrical companies, or groups of actors, came to the colonies from England. Performances in the small theaters of the New World were poorly attended, largely because many churches warned their members against paid public performances. An English preacher named George Whitefield arrived in New York in the 1740s. According to one observer at the time, whenever Whitefield preached at the Presbyterian Church on Wall Street the result was a "suppressing of the usual public amusements." But despite their difficulties finding an audience or a theater in which to play, the acting companies from England usually came up with a way to stage their productions. When the group that performed *Othello* in New York in 1751 toured the colonies, they advertised the play in a way that would appeal to the deeply religious. After all, *Othello* showed that jealousy was evil, didn't it? So, they billed the production as "a moral dialogue in 5 acts."

As the colonial cities grew and prospered, people of different religions came together. This caused many believers to feel less restricted by their religions, and professional theater in America grew. More theaters were built and more touring companies of actors came from England. By the late 1760s a play no longer had to be advertised as moral or uplifting. *The Padlock,* a comic opera by two Englishmen named Isaac Bickerstaffe and Charles Dibdin played to large audiences when it was produced in New York in 1769. One of its characters, a West Indian slave named Mungo, spoke in dialect and was usually drunk. He was played by an Englishman named Lewis Hallam, in "blackface."

By the time of the American Revolution, native-born Americans were writing and acting in plays, although most of their efforts were less than brilliant, to judge by the comments of observers of the day. Some of the best early plays written by Americans contained black characters—either servants or slaves. In 1776, the year the United States declared its independence from Britain, an American playwright named John Leacock produced a play called *The Fall of British Tyranny*. It contained a scene in which a group of escaped slaves board a British man-of-war ship anchored off Norfolk, Virginia. The slaves were all played by whites.

Although most whites saw nothing wrong with white actors playing the roles of black characters, the black people in the American colonies were beginning to feel differently. As the years had passed, and as the population of the colonies had grown, many blacks had become free. Some were former indentured servants—a group of people who had agreed to come to America and work for a certain number of years in exchange for eventual liberty. Others were ex-slaves who had gained their freedom in return for faithful service. Still others had managed to save enough money to buy their freedom. But neither the former indentured servants nor the former slaves were likely to go to the theater. They could not afford the tickets. But they heard about the plays, and it must have bothered them to know that productions written by whites contained black characters when there weren't any black actors to play the parts, and that white actors thought they could play black characters even though they knew very little about black people. It must also have upset them to see blacks portrayed only as slaves or servants when in fact well-to-do and educated blacks were active in many areas of American life.

There were black landowners, and even black slaveowners. Blacks were founding organizations, churches and newspapers. There was even a black, published poet, Phillis Wheatley. Born in Africa and brought to America as a slave at the age of eight, she published her first poem in a newspaper nine years later in 1770. Three years after that, a whole book of her poetry was published in London.

There were black soldiers and heroes, too. In 1770, six years before Leacock's play was produced, Crispus Attucks, a former slave, was killed by British troops in the Boston Massacre. Today, he is called the first American to die in the Revolution.

As the war progressed, whole units of black soldiers were called up to fight the Redcoats. Indeed, the Massachusetts Minutemen included blacks. Yet at war's end, although blacks had helped to win America its independence, they didn't have the power to get an antislavery clause put into the Constitution of the brand-new United States. Therefore, slavery and discrimination against free blacks continued. In terms of theater, this meant that only whites wrote plays and black roles continued to be played by whites in blackface.

In the years immediately following the Revolution, the population of the United States, including its free blacks, expanded rapidly. By the early 1800s, there were enough freemen in some major cities to join together and create the first recorded black theater. Many blacks, slave and free, had felt the need to express themselves creatively on the stage long before the 1820s, but, as we have seen, theater needs an audience, and usually an audience that can pay at least a small admission. With the founding of the African Grove Theatre in New York City in the 1820s, these conditions were finally met. People to write, stage, and act in the plays seemed to appear out of nowhere. In fact, they had been there all along, waiting for their moment to come.

The African Grove Theatre

Dr. James McCune Smith described the beginnings of the African Grove in the October 5, 1861, issue of *The Weekly Anglo-African:*

In 1816–17, Mr. Brown, steward of a Liverpool liner, gave up following the sea, hired a house on the north side of Thomas Street and fitted up a tea garden. In the evening he made the garden attractive by vocal and instrumental music. His brother stewards and their wives and the colored population generally gave him a full share of patronage.

5

Among his artistes [was] . . . James Hewlett. These evening entertainments were not dry affairs. Brandy and gin toddies, wine, porter and strong ale, with cakes and meats, enabled the audience to gratify several senses and appetites at the same time.

James Hewlett was quite a character. A very fine singer, he added dramatic exhibitions to the entertainments. His off nights were invariably spent in the gallery of the old Park Theatre, and spent not in vain, for he soon became celebrated for the talent and versatility which enabled him to perform several widely different characters at one exhibition. He followed the fashionable world to Saratoga. When rival singers would scatter their announcements through the hotels there would appear, tastily printed on white satin:

JAMES HEWLETT
Vocalist and Shakespeare's Proud Representative
Will Give an Entertainment
In Singing and Acting
In the large room of the United States Hotel

So great was Mr. Brown's success with his tea garden that in four or five years he built a theater in Mercer Street. The edifice was of wood, roughly built, having capacity for an audience of three or four hundred. The enterprise was quite successful, the audience being composed largely of laughter-loving young clerks, who came to see the sport, but invariably paid their quarter for admission.

The *"artiste"* cited in Dr. Smith's article, James Hewlett, was a native of Long Island. He is said to have founded the company of actors that performed at Mr. Brown's theater and took its name from Brown's tea garden, the African Grove. All concerned did their best to make this exciting and ambitious venture succeed. As the advertisements said, "neither time nor expense has been spared in rendering this entertainment agreeable to the ladies and gentlemen of color."

The first recorded performance at the African Grove Theatre took place in September 1821. In his book *Black Manhattan,*

James Weldon Johnson reprinted a notice in the newspaper *National Advocate* announcing a production of Shakespeare's *Richard III* by a group of Negro citizens in the "upper apartments of the African Grove." James Hewlett played the title role. In the same month, he also danced the major role in a Negro ballet that he had written and that was praised in the *National Advocate*. This ballet was also probably presented at the African Grove Theatre.

The second recorded performance took place in October 1821. Once again, the *National Advocate* carried the notice and Johnson reprinted it in *Black Manhattan*: "The gentlemen of color announce another play at their Pantheon, corner of Bleecker and Mercer Streets, on Monday evening. They have graciously made a partition at the back of the house, for the accommodation of the whites."

What was this? Blacks making whites sit in the rear? Were the members of the African Grove company seeking revenge because those New York theaters that allowed blacks in at all (most posted signs that said "Dogs and Negroes Forbidden!") seated them in a special back gallery? Probably not. The company was apparently forced to set up this seating arrangement because of the rude behavior of some non-blacks in the audience.

The idea that blacks had dared to start their own theater and were actually performing Shakespeare's plays struck some whites as hilariously funny, and they went to the African Grove to laugh at and mock the players. When the management attempted to seat whites in the rear of the theater because "white people do not know how to behave at entertainment designed for ladies and gentlemen of color," the white hoodlums became even more determined to disrupt the performances. The policemen who arrived to restore order weren't much better than the hoodlums. They would arrest the actors in the middle of a play and put them in jail. Eventually, the African Grove Theatre was forced to close temporarily because of the frequent disturbances.

In the summer of 1823 a white writer attending a performance of Shakespeare's *Othello* at the "African Theatre" described the playhouse as a wooden frame structure with cracks between the boards. He went on to report that the orchestra consisted of a violin, a clarinet and a fiddle played by two white men and one black (the only record that whites were also involved in the entertainment at the African Grove). The audience, he concluded, was composed of "white, black, copper-coloured and light-brown."

On June 20 and June 21, 1823, at the "theatre in Bleecker Street, in the rear of the One Mile Stone, Broadway," (an actual stone marker showing the distance of one mile from City Hall) two special benefit performances were given by the African Company. As recorded by George C. D. Odell in *Annals of the New York Stage,* the playbill for these performances announced: "The Performers of the African Company have kindly united their services in order to contribute a Benefit to their Manager, Mr. Brown, who, for the first time, throws himself on the liberality of a generous public. Mr. Brown trusts that his unrelinquished exertions to please, will be justly considered by the Gentlemen and Ladies of this City, as on them depends his future support, and they can declare whether he is 'To be— or not to be—That is the question.' "

The last quote, from Shakespeare's play *Hamlet,* is spoken by the young prince as he considers whether or not to commit suicide. It is not known what kind of trouble Mr. Brown was in, but if the African Grove Theatre's manager was broke, his establishment couldn't have been doing very well. One thing seems sure: the customers' manners had not improved. The benefit's playbill carried this warning: "Nota bene [Note well]: Proper officers will attend to keep order."

The African Grove Theatre probably closed in 1823 or 1824. Some members of the company went on to start other groups and theaters. A black theater is known to have existed on Marion Street near Houston Street in 1824 and James Hewlett gave a presentation of "Shakespeare's proud heroes" at No. 11 Spruce Street on March 30, 1826. The next year, a visiting Englishwoman named Mrs. Anthony Trollope reported in a letter home that was later reprinted in *The Negro in New York* by Roi Ottley and William Weatherby: "There are a great number of Negroes in New York, all free; their emancipation having been completed in 1827. Not even in Philadelphia, where the antislavery opinions have been most active and violent, do the blacks appear to wear an air of so much consequence as they do in New York. They have several chapels . . . and a theatre in which none but Negroes perform. At this theatre a gallery is appropriated to such whites as choose to visit it . . ."

The full emancipation of 1827 mentioned by Mrs. Trollope had the same effect on those whites opposed to black freedom as salt does when it is rubbed into an open wound. Groups of enraged whites were determined that Negroes would keep their "place" regardless of the law. The number of assaults by whites on blacks increased alarmingly, and in 1829 the city authorities closed all places where blacks were known to congregate because of the danger of "civil discord." These places included all existing black theaters.

In the final analysis the African Grove Theatre represented no more than a small, brief effort on the part of a few idealistic black people to start something for which most black New Yorkers were not ready and that most white New Yorkers were unwilling to allow. Its main importance probably lay in the fact that it was here that Ira Aldridge got his start.

Ira Aldridge

Ira Aldridge was born July 24, 1807. His father, who served as pastor of the black Zion Chapel in New York City, is believed to have been the son of a Senegalese chief. Although his family was not wealthy, Ira was born into better circumstances than were most black children in 1807. He also had the good fortune to attend a free school, African Free School No. 1, in New York City. The Manumission Society, a white group devoted to the freeing of slaves, had founded seven such schools in about 1787 for the education of freeborn black children. In those days, all other schools were tuition schools. There were no free schools for white children. So in one respect, at least, Ira Aldridge was lucky to be black, for otherwise he might never have received a formal education.

Ira apparently became interested in the theater at a very young age, probably through attending performances at those New York theaters that admitted blacks. At theaters like the Park, which faced City Hall, he would have seen the leading Shakespearean actors of the day. He also appears to have gotten a job that took him behind the scenes of the Chatham Theatre, where he was able to get an intimate look at stage life.

Ira is said to have been one of the members of the African Grove Company. It was probably there that he made his first appearance on the stage, playing Rolla, the hero in the play *Pizarro,* about the famous Peruvian Inca leader who tried to defend his people from the invading Spaniards. It must have been a demanding task for a teenager. Aldridge was hardly more than a boy at the time, perhaps 13 or 14 years old.

Ira's father wanted his son to join the clergy and it is said that Ira attended Glasgow University in Scotland, home of the Presbyterian Church and the proper training ground for a future Presbyterian minister. But Ira's love of the theater won out, and he ended up on the London stage. Londoners, and the London theater, were hardly free of racism at the time, but there were opportunities for black actors in some of the city's theaters. The Coburg, where James Hewlett had played, was one of these and it was here that Aldridge got a part in *The Revolt of Surinam, or A Slave's Revenge,* a melodrama based on the life of a tragic black hero named Oroonoko. A handbill which has survived from that performance announced the first-night appearance of a "Tragedian of Colour, from the African Theatre, New York."

Aldridge went from the Coburg to London's Sadler's Wells Theatre, acting in as many plays and playing as many roles as he could. He then toured the English provinces for a number of years, to further perfect his craft. There weren't many blacks in Great Britain in those days and Aldridge came up against racism at times. In Dublin, Ireland, for example, he was banned from the stage until he could talk the theater manager into producing a limited engagement of *Othello*. The play, with Aldridge in the title role, was a smash success. The white British actor Edmund Kean saw the Dublin production and was so impressed that he asked Aldridge to do a touring version of the play with him. Aldridge played Othello to Kean's Iago, the villain who destroys Othello and Desdemona.

It was probably the success of this touring production that allowed Aldridge to bypass the color bar at the prestigious Theatre Royal at Covent Garden in London. With Kean's help the two men opened there in *Othello* on April 10, 1833.

When Kean died later that year, Aldridge decided to leave England. There was more racism in the British theater than he cared to deal with, and he felt certain that a portion of the British press would never take his work seriously. He never regretted his decision to move on. Over the next 30-odd years he played in nearly every European capital and gave command performances for the emperors of Germany and Austria and the crowned heads of Sweden and Russia. He was decorated by the city of Berlin and by the city of Berne in Switzerland. People called him "the African Roscius," after Quintus Roscius Gallus, a famous slave-actor in ancient Rome. That's how far back they had to go to find another black man who'd had such a sensational impact on the theater.

Though *Othello* was Aldridge's favorite play, he appeared in other Shakespearean dramas as well. He played the title roles

Ira Aldridge in Shakespeare's *Titus Andronicus.*

in *King Lear, Hamlet, Richard III* and *Macbeth* as well as Shylock in *The Merchant of Venice.* Since all of these roles were white roles, he played them in whiteface. The French writer Theophile Gautier saw Aldridge play King Lear in St. Petersburg (now

Leningrad) in Russia. According to Gautier, "A white paint covered his cheeks and a great white beard enveloped the rest of his face, descending to his chest. Cordelia, herself, would not have guessed that she had a Negro father." Aldridge played many other roles as well, most of which had never before been played by a black actor. In a letter he wrote to the manager of a French theater on August 24, 1854, and reprinted in *Ira Aldridge, The Negro Tragedian* by Herbert Marshall and Mildred Stock, he mentions his impact on the peoples of Europe:

Sir,

For three years I have toured the principal cities of Germany, Austria, Hungary, where my representations have been crowned with the greatest success. It is unheard of that a person of African nationality should play dramatic roles. The success I have had in the greatest theaters of Germany, has increased my desire to make an attempt in the French capital.

His Majesty, the King of Prussia, has condescended to honor me with the Large Gold Medal for Art and Sciences, the Emperor of Austria with The Medal of Ferdinand, and Switzerland with the White Cross.

My intention is to come to France with a troupe of English players to give the following: Othello, Macbeth, King Lear, Richard III, The Merchant of Venice. I ask for a guarantee to cover the expenses I will have to bring my troupe to Paris. For each performance I ask for half the net receipts or a fixed salary. Waiting for the favor of your prompt reply,

Ira Aldridge, African Tragedian

Aldridge counted many of the rich and famous of Europe among his friends: Richard Wagner, the composer, Jenny Lind, the "Swedish Nightingale," Alexandre Dumas, the black French author of *The Three Musketeers* and *The Count of Monte Cristo.* Hans Christian Andersen was another friend. Andersen wrote many successful stories; but only one successful play, *The Mulatto,* which was inspired by an Aldridge performance.

Aldridge's first wife, an Englishwoman named Margaret, died in 1858, and he married again. His second wife was a Swedish opera singer named Countess Amanda Pauline Brandt. One of their children, Amanda Christine, was a pupil of Jenny Lind and later gave voice lessons in London to a young man named Paul Robeson, who would be compared with her father.

Although Aldridge became a naturalized British subject in 1863, he never forgot his homeland. When slavery was officially abolished at the end of the Civil War, he began planning an American tour, delighted at the thought of returning in triumph to the land of his birth. But before the business arrangements could be completed, Aldridge took ill. He died on August 7, 1867, in Lodz, Poland, where he is buried. His grave is still cared for by the Society of Polish Artists of Film and Theatre.

In 1932, the new Shakespeare Memorial Theatre at Stratford-on-Avon in England, the birthplace of William Shakespeare, was dedicated on the anniversary of the playwright's birthday, April 23. Visitors to Stratford-on-Avon today can see thirty-three seats in that theater bearing bronze plates dedicated to the great actors in world drama. One of these is inscribed simply: IRA ALDRIDGE.

It is extremely unfortunate that Ira Aldridge never made his American tour. The reputation he had made for himself in Europe and the honors he had received there might have helped to change white attitudes toward blacks on the stage. He also might have inspired blacks who were interested in serious drama to form their own theaters. There had been almost no black theater activity since the days of the African Grove, which made it next to impossible for black actors to act and meant that black playwrights had no place to write for. However, one remarkable black man, William Wells Brown, managed not only to get his plays published during the tense years preceding the Civil War, but also to have them presented. True, they were one-man shows performed by Brown himself in lecture halls rather than on stages, but they did much to educate their audiences about their subject matter, slavery, an issue with which their author was well acquainted indeed.

William Wells Brown

William Wells Brown was born in slavery in 1814 in Missouri. He spent most of his youth planning ways to escape to the North. In 1833, at the age of nineteen, he persuaded his mother to flee with him to Canada, but they were caught eleven days later in Illinois. Slavemasters in the middle western states traditionally punished escaped slaves by selling them to the Deep South, from which escape was practically impossible. Brown's mother suffered this fate; he never saw her again after she left on a boat bound for New Orleans. Brown had belonged to a different owner, whose father had made him swear never to sell a slave to the Deep South. Brown's master kept his promise, selling Brown instead to another man in Missouri. The next year, Brown ran away again.

This time he was helped by the newly organized Underground Railroad. When he fell ill in Ohio, the Quaker couple who were hiding him were so kind to him that William took the man's name, Wells Brown.

With the help of many dedicated "conductors" on the Underground Railroad, Brown finally reached Cleveland, Ohio, where he got work on a Lake Erie steamer, married, and began to educate himself. Two years later, he and his wife and their daughter moved to Buffalo, New York. Steamboat work was more plentiful there, the black population was much larger than Cleveland's, and, most important, Buffalo was very close to Canada, which was a haven for fugitive slaves.

Brown was soon deeply involved with various Buffalo antislavery societies. As an escaped slave who could tell his story in an exciting and moving way, he was in great demand as a speaker at antislavery meetings. By 1844 he was listing himself in the City Directories as "William W. Brown, lecturer," and was working as a lecturing agent for the Western New York Anti-Slavery Society. Once during his many travels he was put off a railroad coach by a conductor who said blacks were not permitted to ride in the coaches with white people. Since there were no empty coaches, it was decided that Brown should ride in the open freight car. When the conductor came around to collect the passenger fare, Brown refused to pay. What was the charge to move freight? he asked. Twenty-five cents for 100 pounds, the conductor replied. Brown, who weighed about 150 pounds, promptly handed the conductor 37½¢.

After years of lecturing, Brown decided to write a book. His autobiography was published in Boston, where he had moved with his two daughters after separating from his wife, in June 1849. He would later write other books, including a volume of short biographies of great blacks, stories, and articles for magazines and newspapers. He wrote his first play in 1856.

Brown had learned by experience that it took more than just lecturing to hold the attention of audiences at antislavery meetings and to attract new converts to the cause. He emphasized the evils of slavery by recounting his own early experiences and further spread his message through poetry and song. He was also one of the first black writers to use the dramatic form to get his point across.

Brown's first play was titled *Experience, or, How to Give a Northern Man a Backbone.* It was a farce about a Boston minister who is proslavery until he takes a trip south and somehow manages to be sold into slavery himself. After being cruelly treated, he is eventually freed, and returns home determined to devote himself to the antislavery cause. Brown read the play on many antislavery society platforms, first in and around Boston, and later in New York, Philadelphia and dozens of other cities and towns along the eastern seaboard. Entertaining and different, the work was very well received.

Brown also wrote a second antislavery play called *The Escape; or, A Leap for Freedom: A Drama in Five Acts.* Published in the spring of 1858 by a Boston publisher, it was the first play by a black ever to appear in print.

The play is about slavery, of course. Dr. Gaines, a physician and politician in Missouri, is a man who appreciates beautiful slave women. As the play opens, he is pursuing Melinda, a pretty young slave. He does not know that Melinda is in love with Glen, a fellow slave, or that the two are secretly married. Mrs. Gaines is determined to sell Melinda before the doctor can get involved with her. In order to keep peace with his wife, Dr. Gaines pretends to sell Melinda, but instead hides her in a remote cottage on his plantation.

When Melinda tells her master that she will not abandon her virtue and reveals that she is married, Dr. Gaines is furious. He storms out of the cottage bent on getting Glen thrown into prison. Moments later, his wife, who has discovered Melinda's whereabouts, arrives. She attempts to force Melinda to drink poison, and when Melinda refuses, she tries to stab the girl with a dagger. After a violent struggle, Melinda flees.

Meanwhile, Glen, who has been thrown into prison on Dr. Gaines's orders, escapes from jail. He and Melinda find each other in the forest and set off for Canada and freedom.

Brown read this play to many audiences, and by all accounts it was as well received as his earlier play. It contained some very exciting scenes, a few extremely well-developed characters, and enough good dialogue to hold the attention of audience after audience for the full hour and a quarter it took to read it aloud. Although William Wells Brown's plays were never performed on an actual stage, it must have given him comfort in his later years to know that he had played a part, however small, in bringing about the abolition of slavery.

2
"Why Does a Chicken Cross the Road?"

The Rise and Fall of Minstrelsy in the 1800s

The Civil War did little to improve the lot of black people in America. Although slavery was abolished, no provisions were made to educate and train the newly freed slaves to enjoy the fruits of freedom. Instead, the United States government concentrated on reuniting the country, and such reunification could only be accomplished by returning control of the former Confederate states to the former Confederates. Once southerners got back into power in these states, they made sure that conditions for blacks were, if anything, worse than they had been during slavery.

The abolition of slavery did, however, make it possible for blacks to be admitted onto the white American stage. After the Civil War, blacks were at last able to participate in a form of entertainment called minstrelsy, which owed its very existence to them.

The origins of minstrelsy, the first truly American contribution to the history of theater, can be found in the entertainments provided by slaves on the plantations of the South. Every plantation of any size had its talented slave dancers and comedians and musicians who played the banjo, a genuine black instrument brought over from Africa (in 1784 Thomas Jefferson mentioned in his Journals hearing a slave instrument he called a "banjar") and the bones (animal rib bones, cut, cleaned, and bleached white in the sun, which were used as clappers). Plantation owners enjoyed this entertainment immensely, and treated guests to a special performance by the plantation slave band. At least one enterprising white man realized early-on that money could be made from this kind of entertainment. In 1791 a Negro troupe of comedians and entertainers, under the direction of Louis Tabary, gave performances in New Orleans. Other semi-professional bands of blacks probably toured southern plantations and towns, but there could not have been many. Most blacks were slaves, and slaves were not free to travel.

By the early 1800s some white performers had begun imitating the blacks. Made up with burnt cork, they performed jigs and other dances of English and Irish origin to popular songs about Negroes. Performances by whites in blackface, playing the traditional Negro instruments, even crossed the ocean to England. A comic musical called *Tom and Jerry*, presented on the London stage in 1820, included a funny dance by the characters "African Sal" and "Dusty Bob." According to one source this same musical was performed by the African Company in New York in 1821.

In spite of this early activity, real minstrelsy, focusing on the Negro as a source of theatrical material, did not begin until 1829–1830 when a little-known performer named Thomas Rice happened to see an old black man singing and dancing in the stable behind the theater where Rice was performing. A man who claimed to have been an eyewitness to this historic moment described the scene this way to Marshall W. Stearns, author of *The Story of Jazz:*

As was usual with slaves, they called themselves after their owner, so that old Daddy had assumed the name of Jim Crow. He was very much deformed, the right shoulder being drawn up high, the left leg

Poster announcement for the musical *Tom and Jerry*.

stiff and crooked at the knee, giving him a painful, but at the same time laughable limp. He used to croon a queer old tune with words of his own, and at the end of each verse would give a little jump, and when he came down he set his 'heel a-rockin'.' He called it 'jumping Jim Crow.' The words of the refrain were:

> *"Wheel about, turn about,*
> *Do jis so,*
> *An' ebry time I wheel about,*
> *I jump Jim Crow!"*

Rice thought Crow's performance was hilarious, and he decided to take on not just the old man's comical song and dance but also his name. Thomas Rice became known professionally as Daddy "Jim Crow" Rice. He was an immediate hit, and his act spawned dozens of imitations. The words Jim Crow would later come to mean any sort of discrimination against black people.

In 1843 what may have been the first real minstrel show took place at the Bowery Amphitheatre in New York. It featured four actors who performed popular skits and songs in blackface, calling themselves the Virginia Minstrels. Other groups, like Buffalo's Christy Minstrels, (who would later claim that they were the original minstrel troupe) sprang up almost simultaneously in several cities and were immediately popular among all classes of people. In March 1847, for example, Christy's Minstrels performed at the exclusive New York Society Library. As the New York *Tribune* reported on March 12th, "Many of the most fashionable families attend, as the performances are a pleasing relief to the high toned excitement of the Italian Opera. Negro melodies are the very democracy of music."

A group called the Ethiopian Serenaders played before President John Tyler at the White House in 1844. By the mid-1850s there were at least ten major minstrel houses in New York City. When Commodore Perry forced his fleet into Japan in 1853, his crew chose to introduce the Japanese to American culture by putting on a minstrel show. Before long, all minstrel shows were following the same basic three act formula.

In the first act of the show, Negroes (whites in blackface) were seated on a row of chairs onstage. An "interlocutor" or "straight man," placed in the middle of the line, went through a series of humorous exchanges with the two "end men," called Tambo and Bones. The humor was very childish and full of puns. Here is one famous example:

END MAN: *"Why did the chicken cross the road?"*
INTERLOCUTOR: *"I don't know. Why?"*
END MAN: *"To get to the other side!"*

The second part of the show was called the "olio," which means mixture or variety. It included songs and dances, banjo-playing, performing dogs or monkeys, and just about any other kind of act that the group members could come up with.

The third act, called the "after-piece," also featured variety entertainment. It sometimes included take-offs on popular plays, operas and important persons. A device called the "stump speech," which mocked pretentious people, whether pompous white politicians or "uppity" city blacks, was an audience favorite. The following speech, delivered by a black-faced character in an ill-fitting suit with a too-short tie and too-big shoes, was given as an example by Robert C. Toll in a 1978 article in *American Heritage*: "Transcendentalism is dat spiritual cognosence ob psychological irrefragibility, connected wid conscientient ademption ob incolumbient spirituality . . . dat became ana-tomi-cati-cally tattalable in de cir-cum ambulation commotion ob ambiloquous voluminiousness."

From start to finish, the shows depended on the Negro, or at least on whites' images of the Negro. The instruments were traditional instruments preferred by blacks. The dances and the songs were imitations of black dances and songs, and the dialogue was an imitation of black language. And, of course, the

"Gentlemen, be seated." The first part of the show always ended with a spirited "walk-around," as each individual performer got up, pranced around the stage, and then did a jig. Part two, the olio, featuring the usual variety acts, was followed by the finale, a group song or dance or combination of both. The major difference between minstrel shows of the 1860s and those of the 1840s was that the later shows had more people and less freshness.

A second important difference was in the performers' portrayals of blacks. Minstrelsy had remained primarily a southern-based form of entertainment, and white southerners blamed blacks to a great extent for the war and its effect on the southern way of life. Therefore, whatever sympathy had been shown on stage for slave ways of speaking and behaving before the war was replaced in the postwar years by the creation of three Negro stereotypes that still exist in the minds of some whites today.

The first sterotype was of the southern Negro: a happy-go-lucky soul, full of "natural rhythm," who shuffles his feet, loves watermelon, and has no ambition to leave the plantation, knowing that he is best off under massa's care. The second stereotype was of the southern black who had made the mistake of leaving the plantation and going North. He is ignorant and bumbling and hasn't a chance of surviving in the new environment. It is plain that he would be much better off back on the farm. The third stereotype is of the northern "dandy," who over-dresses and thinks of nothing but women and good times. He has a ridiculous name like Count Julius Caesar Mars Napoleon Sinclair Brown and is given to talking in "stump speech" style.

When black minstrel troupes were finally able to come together and perform, they found themselves stuck with these stereotypes. They even had to perform in blackface! Audiences were accustomed to seeing minstrels with burnt cork on their faces, and it didn't matter if those faces were naturally black to begin with. Audiences were *used* to seeing minstrels with

white actors were made up and dressed to look like blacks, or more exactly to look the way whites *thought* blacks looked.

All in all, during the pre-Civil War period, the image of blacks presented on the minstrel stage by white performers in blackface was not unsympathetic. The characters were portrayed as human beings and there was a sort of unspoken admiration for the rhythms and the dances and the humor of the Negro. This sympathy was probably increased in some parts of the country after the publication of Harriet Beecher Stowe's book *Uncle Tom's Cabin* in 1852, but even old Tom's story was not enough to move white audiences or white minstrel troupes to admit blacks onto the stage. For the most part, blacks remained barred from minstrelsy and barred from the theaters where minstrel shows were presented. But there were exceptions. In some of the northern cities where the abolitionist cause was strong black performers were welcomed. In 1858, a touring group billed as the "Extraordinary SEVEN SLAVES, Just from Alabama, who are now earning their freedom by giving concerts under the guidance of their Northern friends and guarantees," performed in Springfield, Massachusetts. The handbill advertising the show boasted: "Immense success—8000 people in two days at the Broadway Tabernacle, New York." The seven were called, appropriately enough for the time, Boy William, Boy Thomas, Boy Francis, Boy George, Boy John and so forth. In the mid-ninteenth century only one young man, "Juba," seems to have gained acceptance in the South as well as the North, on white stages and black, and on the same stage with white performers.

Juba (William Henry Lane)

As is often the case with blacks, famous or not, prior to this century, there is no record of Juba's birth, parents or early years. He was probably born around 1825, most likely free. Legend has it that he learned much of his dancing art from

"Uncle" Jim Lowe, a black jig and reel dancer who was never permitted on the stages of regular theaters and so had to confine his performances to saloons and dance halls.

At first the young William Lane was limited to dancing for a supper of fried eels and ale. But thanks to his outstanding talent he was soon in New York dancing in black-operated dance halls that billed him as "Master Juba." His stage name probably derived from a popular dance based on an African step-dance called Giouba, a kind of elaborate jig. A feature writer for the New York *Herald* described one of these early performances:

At the time when he performed at Pete Williams', in Orange Street, New York, those who passed through the long hallway and entered the dance hall . . . saw this phenomenon, 'Juba,' imitate all the dancers of the day and their special steps. Then Bob Ellingham, the interlocutor and master of ceremonies, would say, 'Now, Master Juba, show your own jig.' Whereupon he would go through all his own steps and specialties, with never a resemblance in any of them to those he had just imitated.

By 1845, Juba was touring with three white minstrels, billed as the Ethiopian Minstrels. Advertised as "The Greatest Dancer in the World!" he became so famous that Master John Diamond, a well-known white dancer, began to worry. Diamond challenged Juba to a series of dance contests held primarily in New York. Juba apparently won them all, or so his billing boasted.

Juba next toured New England with the Georgia Champion Minstrels. Handbills for the show advertised him as: "The Wonder of the World, Juba, Acknowledged to be the Greatest Dancer in the World. Having danced at the Chatham Theatre for $500, and at the Bowery Theatre for the same amount, and established himself as the King of All Dancers. No conception can be formed of the variety of beautiful and intricate steps exhibited by him with ease. You must see to believe."

The young performer went on to join the famous Pell's Ethiopian Serenaders in London. He took the city by storm. All kinds of critical praise survives, but the words of the critic in the *Theatrical Times* of August 1848 are especially worth quoting:

The performances of this young man are far above the common performances of the [fakers] who give imitations of American and Negro character; there is an ideality in what he does that makes his effort at once grotesque and poetical, without losing sight of the reality of representation.

Juba took time from his busy professional schedule to marry an English girl, but his marriage was short, as was his life. He died in London in 1852, well before the age of thirty.

Few have heard of Juba today. But in the middle of the last century he was one of the world's greatest dancers and the one black performer who was allowed on the white minstrel stage.

It was not until after the Emancipation Proclamation and the end of the Civil War that black performers in any appreciable number could appear on the minstrel stage. By then minstrelsy had unfortunately been reduced to a formula that nobody bothered to question. Since few blackface minstrels now visited plantations to study black music, dancing, and humor, there was no energy or life to their imitations. The wit, imagination, and brightness of early minstrelsy had given way to a standard, unimaginative routine, making minstrelsy a caricature of its former self.

The structure of the postwar minstrel show closely followed that of the prewar productions. In the opening, or part one, at least seventeen men in elaborate costumes sat in a line, their faces blackened with burnt cork. In the center was the traditional interlocutor, with Mr. Tambo and Mr. Bones at the ends. The performance always began with the interlocutor saying,

their lips painted white and sometimes outlined with red to make them look thicker. If black minstrels didn't make up as expected, they wouldn't look like minstrels. In their appearance and in their performance, they were forced to do what amounted to an imitation of an imitation of plantation slave life.

Still, the black minstrels were able to bring about some changes in the old, tired minstrelsy formula. They added freshness to the jokes about themselves (people usually make better jokes about themselves than other people make about them), they introduced new dances, and they brought a new kind of music, based on black folk dancing, that would come to be called "ragtime." Several black minstrel groups became successful and famous because of the imagination and creativity they brought to the minstrel show format. One of the first of these innovative troupes was the Georgia Minstrels.

The Georgia Minstrels

This successful all-black ensemble was organized in 1865, probably in Georgia, by a black man named Charles Hicks. The group consisted of well-trained musicians, and audiences seemed to like them. But it was very hard for the black manager of a black minstrel group to deal with southern theater managers, who were invariably white, in those days. After two or three troublesome years, Hicks took on a white man, Charles Callender, as his booking agent. Before long Callender had taken over management of the group, which became known as Callender's Original Georgia Minstrels. It included Billy Kersands, who would become the most famous dancer and comedian of his day, and Horace (sometimes referred to as Howard) Weston, one of the very few black solo performers who was allowed on white stages at this time.

Many others in the group were as talented and accomplished as Kersands and Weston. James Trotter, author of a book called *Music and Some Highly Musical Musicians*, wrote in 1877:

At least four of their number have been in the past accomplished teachers of music; one has played in some of the best orchestras in England; one is a superior performer upon at least four instruments, while he is a fair player of twelve; several others are excellent performers on two or three instruments; and three of the troupe arrange and write music.

Callender's Original Georgia Minstrels ran into financial trouble in the late 1870s. Desperate, Gustave Frohman, the manager at the time, decided to add a performance of Harriet Beecher Stowe's *Uncle Tom's Cabin* to the troupe's repertory. Ever since the novel had been published in 1852, plays based on the story had been performed almost constantly by one white company or another in nearly every city. Frohman decided it was time a group of black performers did the same thing. Some historians say that is how Sam Lucas, a talented troupe member who survived on the stage long after minstrelsy fell from favor, came to be the first black ever to play the role of the black character Uncle Tom. Others, like historian Edith Isaacs, say that Howard Weston was the first. Weston, after playing from 1876 to 1878 on the showboat *Plymouth Rock* operated by two whites named Jarrett and Palmer, went with their *Uncle Tom* company to England and was an enormous hit. He then made a tour of Berlin, Breslau, Vienna, Hamburg and several cities in France—a tour that would have been rare even for a white performer in those days.

Unfortunately, adding *Uncle Tom's Cabin* to the repertory of Callender's Original Georgia Minstrels did little to change the company's fortunes. The group was on the verge of disbanding when a man named Jack Haverly bought it in 1878. Haverly, a great showman with a liking for stage extravaganzas, was famous for presenting huge blackface minstrel shows, both in America and in England. Now he'd decided to do the same thing with an "all-colored" production. Under the name of Haverly's European Minstrels, the troupe opened at Her Majesty's

BILLY KERSANDS

Billy Kersands.   (MUSEUM OF THE CITY OF NEW YORK)

Theatre in London July 1881. It was the biggest minstrel show ever to appear on a British stage, with sixty-five performers onstage, including sixteen end men, eight Tambos and eight Bones. The cast included both women and children, an unheard of thing in minstrelsy, and everyone was dressed in extravagant costumes. Billy Kersands did comic routines. The composer James Bland sang his song "O Dem Golden Slippers." The Bohee Brothers, James and George, the first real banjo virtuosi, played solos and duets and, dressed in velvet coats, knee breeches and jockey hats, performed a double banjo song and dance that became famous. The show was the talk of London, and later toured England's major cities.

In the meantime, the Frohmans, three white brothers, who had managed the Callender Minstrels for a time back in the 1870s, had taken over the management of Madison Square Garden in New York. When they decided to assemble a huge black minstrel company to tour the United States, one of the brothers was sent to Europe to buy the company from Haverly. Billed as Callender's Consolidated Spectacular Colored Minstrels, the group toured the United States for a couple of years before again playing London and the provinces. When the group returned to the United States for the second time, James Bland remained behind and was a phenomenal success in England for twenty years. It is said that he earned $10,000 a year just from performing. Tragically, he died penniless in America in 1911.

Callender's Consolidated Spectacular Colored Minstrels continued, in one form or another, for another decade before falling victim to the changing musical tastes of the country. During its complicated history, this troupe served as an important training ground and base for several of the most talented and famous black minstrels of the post Civil War era.

Other successful black minstrel troupes sprang up after the Civil War. Among the best known were Brooker and Clayton's

Georgia Minstrels, who billed themselves as "The Only Simon Pure Negro Troupe in the World," Lew Johnson's Plantation Minstrel Company, the Hicks and Sawyer Minstrels (the same Hicks who started the Georgia Minstrels), the Richards and Pringle Minstrels and the McCabe and Young Minstrels. But none of the black minstrel troupes ever achieved the fame or success of the white minstrel troupes.

The minstrel rage began to die out around 1890, but minstrelsy itself survived for much longer. Individual entertainers, both white and black, carried the tradition into vaudeville. The superb black entertainer Bert Williams was still doing comedy in blackface up to 1922. The white singer Al Jolson was famous as a blackface performer until 1940, and the white comedian Eddie Cantor carried the tradition along until his death in 1954. Groups, too, continued to give minstrel shows well into this century, especially the black troupes that toured the small towns in the South. This writer remembers visits to his small Alabama hometown by a black minstrel group called Silas Green from New Orleans, who were still active well into the 1950s.

As the twentieth century began, however, performers and groups like the above were the exception rather than the rule. Americans had grown tired of minstrelsy, and it seems that they'd grown tired of seeing blacks on the stage. By now, the South had passed repressive "Jim Crow" laws, and most whites in the North seemed ready to go back to the way things were before the war. Abolitionist fervor had died away along with commitment to black rights.

As part of this discouraging trend white theatrical performers had become tired of sharing their stages with blacks. An item that appeared in the New York *Sun* around 1894 serves to bear this out. It concerned a singer at a New York roof garden who although black was billed as "Koo-i-baba, the Hindoo baritone." There was so much prejudice against "niggers," the theater manager told the *Sun* reporter, that unless the singer could be advertised as a "Hindoo" or "some other dusky foreigner" it would "burst [sic] up his show." The reporter went on to say, "What then can be the fate of the aspiring Negro singer, reciter, or actor in the face of such prejudice among people who began fighting thirty-three years ago to set him free and put him upon an equality with the whites of the South?"

This attitude on the part of white northerners was a terrible blow to the thousands of black entertainers who had been inspired and encouraged by the chance that minstrelsy had offered. Once again, the New York *Sun* recorded the situation:

That there is no lack of Negro talent was recently demonstrated by a well-known minstrel manager, who intends this season to take out a company composed of half Negro and half white minstrels. He advertised in the dramatic weeklies for forty colored persons who could either sing, dance, play the banjo and bones, or tell a funny story. They were to call on Twenty-second street near Broadway at 10 A.M.

At the hour named Twenty-second street was jammed with colored persons waiting to display their various talents to the manager. It was estimated that at least 2,000 had congregated, for many left before the 1,012 first comers had registered their names and addresses with the managers.

Several hotels and barber shops thought that their employees had all gone on strike when they rushed out at 10 o'clock to register their names and addresses with the minstrel managers.

The managers were Primrose and West. The show was called *The Forty Whites and Thirty Blacks,* but it was hardly an example of integration. It was really two shows: a black show about "minstrelsy as it was" and a white second show about "minstrelsy as it is." Each show had its own stage manager, and the black and white actors traveled separately and stayed in separate lodgings whenever possible.

There never was a time during the height of minstrelsy when blacks were completely accepted on white stages or given credit for anything but a "natural" humor and ability to sing and dance. Although, as the article in the New York *Sun* proves, there were thousands of black performers hoping to get into a minstrel show, only a few ever made it, and only a handful were successful enough so that their names survive.

Looking back at how they had to behave on the minstrel stage, it's hard to imagine how these black performers could have wanted any part of minstrelsy. Robert C. Toll, author of two books on minstrelsy, provided some important quotes from the performers themselves in a 1978 article in *American Heritage*. A black minstrel named Tom Fletcher once explained, "It was a big break [for blacks] when show business started. Salaries were not large, but they still amounted to much more than [blacks] were getting . . . and there was the added advantage of opportunity to travel . . ." Besides, there were ways to maintain one's private dignity even while publicly acting the fool. When a young black man asked the legendary Billy Kersands how he could put a whole cup and saucer or three billiard balls into his mouth in front of whites, Kersands replied, "Son, if they hate me, I'm still whipping them, because I'm making them laugh."

3
"Coontown" and Cakewalks

The Black Musical Show, 1890–1916

As the nineteenth century came to a close, certain black entertainers used the experience they had received in minstrelsy to lay the foundations for the modern musical comedy.

According to some historians, the origins of this new theatrical form date back to around 1890, when Sam T. Jack came up with the idea of a show that would glorify black women. Jack, a well-known, white theater-circuit manager, called together some very talented blacks, including the actor Sam Lucas, to assist him in writing and staging the show. He also hired a chorus of sixteen of the most beautiful black girls he could find.

Jack's *Creole Show* was basically a minstrel show. But it differed from the standard format in two ways. In part one there were girls in the center of the line and the interlocutor was a female. More important, the show had an underlying theme—a tribute to the black woman—which set it apart from traditional minstrelsy.

Creole Show was a great success. It opened in Chicago in 1891 and played at Jack's Opera House there during the whole season of the World's Fair in 1893. Moving on to New York, it drew large audiences at the Standard Theatre in Greeley Square, which was close enough to the Broadway theater district to make the run of a black show there cause quite a stir. It did well enough to cause John W. Isham, a black man and a booking agent for the show, to decide to produce a similar show himself.

Isham's show, called *The Octoroons,* also emphasized black women. Organized in New York and produced in 1895, it too followed the basic minstrel pattern. But like *Creole Show* it had a basic underlying theme, and in fact a stronger one than Sam Jack's production. Another unusual feature was that it closed with a medley of opera songs. The next show Isham produced, which was called *Oriental America,* was the first black show to play on Broadway. It made a further progression toward the form we now know as musical comedy and led up to the first black production to break with the minstrel pattern altogether.

A black composer named Bob Cole was responsible for this first completely nonminstrel show, *A Trip to Coontown.* He had gotten involved in writing black musical productions when he was hired by two men named Voelckel and Nolan to write a show for a popular singer named Sissieretta Jones. Known as the "Black Patti," Jones had been appearing on concert stages, singing operatic music. The show Cole wrote for her, *Black Patti Troubadours,* was produced in the same season as *Oriental America.* It followed the minstrel pattern in a general way, and it would play successfully for a number of years, especially in the South.

During the show's first season in New York, Bob Cole asked Voelckel and Nolan for more money. When his request was refused, Cole picked up his musical score and walked out. The managers had him arrested for stealing and he was forced to return the music. This experience convinced Cole that he must find a way to write shows that would make money for him instead of others. He began working on *A Trip to Coontown* with the help of some highly talented fellow blacks: Sam Lucas, who was to be featured in the show, and director Jesse Shipp.

Poster announcement for the *Black Patti Troubadours* starring Sissieretta Jones. (MUSEUM OF THE CITY OF NEW YORK)

A Trip to Coontown opened at the Third Avenue Theatre in 1898. It was a real trailblazer: the first show to be entirely organized, written, produced, and managed by blacks. It was also the first musical show with an overall plot that carried the cast of characters from beginning to end.

Bob Cole went on to coauthor the first two black operettas, or musical plays, *The Shoofly Regiment* (1906) and *Red Moon* (1908), with J. Rosamond Johnson. The two men might have written many more shows together if Cole had not died at a very young age.

The turn of the century was a busy time for black theater, especially in New York. In 1898, the year that *A Trip to Coontown* opened, another group of talented blacks presented a short musical play at the Casino Roof Garden. Called *Clorindy—The Origin of the Cakewalk,* its music was composed by Will Marion Cook, with lyrics by Paul Laurence Dunbar. Ernest Hogan, a well-known black comedian, was the star. The following summer a second musical playlet composed by Cook, *Jes Lak White Folks,* opened at the New York Winter Garden. It was also during this period that Worth's Museum at Sixth Avenue and Thirtieth Street became the home of a black stock company, where twelve to fifteen men and women presented plays. Bob Cole would later head that company, acting as both playwright and stage manager. Many new names and faces were emerging as the twentieth century began, but none were more influential than a team of Negro blackface comedians named Bert Williams and George Walker.

Williams and Walker

Egbert Williams was born in the Bahamas in 1876, but grew up in Riverside, California. He was studying civil engineering in San Francisco when he decided to go into the theater.

George Walker had left high school in his home town, Lawrence, Kansas, to follow a group of black minstrels. He went

George Walker.   (MUSEUM OF THE CITY OF NEW YORK)

from musical show to minstrel show to medicine show to circus, finally ending up in San Francisco. In 1893, he and Williams met and decided to form a team. Williams, who had a fine voice and could play almost any instrument, would be the singer and the "straight man." Walker, a gifted comedian, would dance and play the fool. But the two young men soon realized that they were funnier when they reversed roles, so Walker became the straight man—dressed a little too high-style and spending all the money he could borrow or trick out of the lazy, careless, unlucky Williams—and Williams became the bumbling, sorrowful, comical-in-spite-of-himself patsy.

Williams and Walker realized that they needed some sort of gimmick to get themselves known. After some thought they hit on the ideal solution. There were many teams of white performers at the time who made good money appearing in blackface. As Walker later wrote in *Theatre* magazine, "We finally decided, as white men with black faces were billing themselves 'coons,' Williams and Walker would do well to bill themselves the 'Two Real Coons,' and so we did."

The gimmick worked. The team became very popular in West Coast theaters, where minstrel-type variety shows were now being called vaudeville. By 1896 they had been invited to New York to appear in a production called *The Gold Bug* at the Casino Theatre. The show folded very quickly, but it played long enough for Williams and Walker to be noticed. Koster and Bials, managers of a popular theater, hired them and they played a record run of twenty-eight weeks. During this time they made the cakewalk fashionable.

Invented by blacks, the cakewalk had supposedly gotten its name from the prize awarded at dance contests. It was already popular among the lower- and middle-class whites who went to the bars and saloons where ragtime was played. But the dance had not yet been picked up by high society. Thanks to Williams and Walker, some of the biggest names in New York society now started to "cakewalk" and became skilled at it. The two men, always quick to recognize a possible gimmick, decided to challenge one of the big-name people to a cakewalk contest. In January 1898, they delivered a written challenge to the home of the millionaire William K. Vanderbilt, offering to wager fifty dollars that they could defeat him in a cakewalk competition. Vanderbilt did not respond.

After an unsuccessful attempt to launch themselves and the cakewalk in London, the two men returned to the United States. Their next successful show, *The Sons of Ham,* contained a song called "I'm a Jonah Man," written by Williams and a black composer named Alex Rogers, which would practically become Williams's trademark. The title refers to Jonah in the Bible, who got swallowed by a whale. During the time of slavery, blacks had come to refer to any hard-luck type as a "Jonah man" and this was the type of character Williams portrayed— a sad, discouraged fellow for whom nothing ever goes right, who walks with a shuffle and speaks in the dialect of an ignorant southern black. The cultivated Williams, so well-spoken offstage, played the character so well that he was trapped in it for the rest of his life on the stage.

Perhaps the most important moment in Williams and Walker's career was the day they decided to team up with playwright Will Marion Cook and director Jesse Shipp. The four men proved to be an unbeatable combination. Their first joint venture, a musical play called *In Dahomey,* opened in 1902.

Williams and Walker had been thinking about incorporating African themes and African characters into an American show ever since 1893, when visitors to a San Francisco fair had flocked to see an African troupe from Dahomey. As Walker wrote in *Theatre* magazine in 1906, he and Williams "were not long in deciding that if we ever reached the point of having a show of our own, we would delineate and feature African characters as far as we could and still remain American, and make our acting interesting and entertaining to American audiences." The first of its kind, *In Dahomey* was a comic show

(From left to right) Bert Williams, Adah Walker, and George Walker in a scene from *In Dahomey.* (MUSEUM OF THE CITY OF NEW YORK)

with original music, a story worked out from beginning to end, and elaborate scenery and props. Williams and Walker played two detectives from Boston, Shylock Homestead and Rareback Pinkerton, who are hired by Cicero Lightfoot, president of the Dahomey Colonization Society, to find a lost silver casket. During their search for the casket, the detectives befriend an African king in Dahomey. Later, when they are in danger of being executed by an unfriendly tribe, the king saves them. If the production brings to mind the old Bing Crosby and Bob Hope "On the Road" movies, that is probably no accident. The Crosby/Hope films may well have been inspired by Williams and Walker shows like *In Dahomey.*

In Dahomey made black theatrical history as the first black show ever to *open* on Broadway. It was so successful at the New York Theatre in Times Square that several London theater managers proposed importing the show to England. After their earlier failure in London, Williams and Walker weren't sure that was a good idea. But they decided to give it a try. In the spring of 1903 *In Dahomey* opened at the Shaftsbury Theatre. It received only a lukewarm reception, but fortunately the man who arranged command performances at Buckingham Palace decided it was the perfect show to present at the Prince of Wales's ninth birthday party. Naturally, any play that was presented at the Palace was a play that Londoners wanted to see. They flocked to the Shaftsbury Theatre and the show ran for six more months. It went on to tour the British provinces and France, leaving thousands of new cakewalk lovers in its wake. Apparently, Europe just hadn't been ready for the cakewalk before.

In Dahomey was followed by *In Abyssinia,* which opened at the Majestic Theatre in New York in 1906. This time the two comedians go through all sorts of mishaps in the process of leading a group of pilgrims from Kansas to Jerusalem by way of Addis Ababa. What is important about both these shows is the new subject matter they introduced to black productions. The African settings made it possible to work with much richer cultural and historical material than the old minstrel forms had allowed. While continuing to play American Negro stereotypes, Williams and Walker could interact with elegant African kings and powerful African warriors, showing in the process not all blacks were either dandies or "Jonah men."

Unfortunately, the two men had to be *very* subtle in their methods. Though privately the two believed, as Walker once said, "Nothing seemed more absurd than to see a colored man making himself ridiculous in order to portray himself," they could not boldly cast aside the traditional view of blacks. The white public would not have stood for it, and it was whites who bought the tickets and caused the shows to earn money. There were very strict limits within which Williams and Walker could operate. They had to take heart in the idea that they and their work were at least bringing about *some* changes.

In addition to introducing African locales and characters in their shows, Williams and Walker also introduced what they referred to as Americanized African songs, like "My Zulu Babe," "My Castle on the Nile," and "My Dahomian Queen." But after a time they decided they were relying too heavily on things African. For their third show with Cook and Shipp they chose an American setting. *Bandana Land,* which opened in 1908, was the story of a small-town southern-born minstrel comic who finds out he has inherited a fortune. He returns to his home town to claim his inheritance only to find that everyone, black and white, is scheming to deprive him of it. In the end, he manages to outwit the plotters in clever and comical ways. This show, too, was a big success, but George Walker fell ill during its run and it was hard for Bert Williams to go on without him. The two were a perfect team, and depended heavily on each other. As it turned out, George Walker never appeared on the stage again.

In the same year Bert Williams opened in a new show called *Mr. Lode of Kole,* but it didn't have the same excitement as the old productions. Williams admitted that without his partner he felt "like a rudderless ship." So when Abraham Erlanger, producer of the Ziegfeld Follies, invited him to join that company, he accepted the offer.

The Ziegfeld Follies were already famous. Started by Florenz Ziegfeld, they were huge extravaganzas, packed with beautiful chorus girls, elaborate costumes and sets and talented variety acts. Until Bert Williams's arrival the company had been all white. Williams integrated the Ziegfeld Follies and a special role was written into the show for him.

The rest of the cast threatened to strike if they had to appear on the same stage with Williams. In desperation Erlanger worked out a compromise: Williams would perform on the stage alone. This was fine with Bert. He went out, did his monologue, and literally stopped the show. The audience applauded and cheered so much that the next act couldn't go on. In no time at all, the rest of the cast decided they wanted very much to appear on stage with Bert Williams! But he was still segregated offstage, riding freight elevators when the rest rode passenger elevators, unable to stay in the same hotels or eat in the same restaurants as the rest of the cast, and suffering all the other indignities of being black in America at that time. As he often said, "It is no disgrace to be a Negro but it is very inconvenient."

Williams remained with the Ziegfeld Follies for ten frustrating years. He dreamed of doing a serious play, but the white public, with whom his popularity grew each year, only seemed to want to see him in his Jonah Man character. At the end of his first three-year contract with the Follies, Williams was offered the chance to perform in a serious play written just for him. He wanted very much to accept the offer, but was held back by his sense of loyalty to Abraham Erlanger and Florenz Ziegfeld for putting a black performer in the Follies. He also realized that if he left Ziegfeld's show there would be no blacks at all on the downtown white stage. In fact, from 1913 to 1917 he was the only black artist working on Broadway. As he said, "We've got our foot in the door, we mustn't let it close again."

Williams finally did leave the Follies when George Le Maire, the white manager of the Winter Garden, offered him much more money and his name in lights to appear in a revue called *Broadway Brevities.* Later, he played the lead in an otherwise all-white musical comedy called *Under the Bamboo Tree* produced by the famous Shubert theater family. Williams's career was cut tragically short. He died of pneumonia at the age of forty-six.

Bert Williams's greatest contributions to the history of black theater were made in his early years when he and George Walker tried to challenge the stereotypes formed during the minstrel era. Although Williams had to go back to the stereotypes after Walker's death, at least he was on a major stage, a solo performer in otherwise all-white shows. At the 1981 Inaugural Gala preceding President Reagan's swearing-in, actor Ben Vereen paid tribute to the legendary song-and-dance man in a rousing minstrel-style routine.

In the end, Williams paid a huge price for his success in

Bert Williams.　　　　(MUSEUM OF THE CITY OF NEW YORK)

the white entertainment world. Unable to use much of his tremendous talent because he was bound to the role he portrayed so well, he was nevertheless the object of jealousy on the part of white and black performers alike. The great comedian W. C. Fields described Williams well when he called him "the funniest man I ever saw; the saddest man I ever knew."

Bandana Land was not only Williams and Walker's last show together, it was also the last successful black show to appear on or near Broadway for nearly a decade.

The twentieth century had gotten off to a bad start in terms of race relations. In the summer of 1900, a fight between a white man and a black man on the corner of Eighth Avenue and 41st Street in New York had resulted in the death of the white man and a rampage against blacks by a huge white mob. It had been a terrifying time for black New Yorkers, including those black entertainers who were supposed to be popular with whites. "Get Ernest Hogan!" the mob cried. "Get Williams and Walker! Get Cole and Johnson!" These were the only blacks the mob knew by name. They massed outside the clubs and theaters where those entertainers were appearing. George Walker had barely managed to escape. Ernest Hogan had been forced to stay in the theater all night. Instead of trying to help blacks who were being beaten by the mob, the white police had joined in the beating.

Nevertheless, there was great activity and great hope in the area of black theater between 1900 and 1910, at least in New York City. But this all changed when Jack Johnson became the first black heavyweight champion of the world. Many whites hated the idea of a black champion, especially a black champion who had shown a marked preference for white women. In 1910 Jim Jeffries, a former title holder, came out of retirement just to win the title away from Johnson. When Johnson beat the "great white hope," as Jeffries was called, it was just too much for many white New Yorkers to take. They rioted in the black sections of Manhattan, beating every black person in sight and destroying many of the businesses that served the black neighborhoods. This caused many blacks to move themselves and their businesses up to Harlem, where the first large concentration of black Manhattanites was forming.

The aftermath of the 1910 riots was distrust between the races, and that wasn't good for the black presence on the white downtown stage. Another reason for the lack of blacks on the stage at that time was the early and almost simultaneous deaths of Ernest Hogan, Bob Cole and George Walker, and Bert Williams's decision to go to the Ziegfeld Follies. These men were not only performers and creators of shows, they also managed their companies. Without their business sense, it was a struggle to keep the companies operating, and without their big names it was hard to get bookings in the major theaters.

Fortunately for black theater, the rise in the black populations of major cities during this uneasy period helped keep the momentum going by providing a large audience to support black community theaters. One of the first of these, the Pekin in Chicago, was opened in 1902. By 1922, there were nine black theaters in Washington, D.C., the biggest of which was the Howard. The second biggest, the Lincoln, had a seating capacity of over two thousand and cost over half a million dollars to build. Philadelphia had two black theaters, the Standard and the Dunbar; Richmond and Norfolk, Virginia, each had three; and there were two each in New Orleans and Chicago. All of them were devoted strictly to theatrical presentations; as motion pictures came into being, special movie theaters were established to house film shows.

The rise of these theaters naturally was accompanied by the rise of black theatrical companies. Among the earliest and best of these were the Pekin Players and the Lafayette and Lincoln Theatres' stock companies.

The Pekin Players

In the early 1900s in Chicago a group of talented young blacks tired of vaudeville and musical comedy decided to get together and read serious dramatic plays aloud, each taking a part. The evenings proved to be so enjoyable that members of the group invited their entertainer friends, and pretty soon there were about 30 black men and women taking part in them. When eleven group members decided to approach the management of the Pekin Theatre about presenting plays there, the Pekin Players were born.

The troupe, founded in 1906, presented "refined white comedies." They made up accordingly. Some of the actors and actresses were so light-skinned that they needed no makeup; the others thought nothing of acting in "whiteface" to make their performances more realistic. Word soon got around Chicago's black community that a company of blacks was presenting serious plays. Many whites thought this was highly amusing and visited the Pekin Theatre in order to have a good laugh. Instead, they found to their great surprise that the performances were quite good and many of them wound up applauding the cast. As one member of the first Pekin Players put it, "We proved to them that negroes *can* act. Even the critics admitted it."

The Pekin Players did comparatively well at the Pekin Theatre. Naturally, they didn't make the same salaries as actors in white theatrical companies, but they made enough to live on. Buoyed by their success, they decided to make a road tour. Nine of the eleven in the company's original cast set out for a theater in New Orleans, where their manager had booked them for fourteen weeks. For a month they played to packed houses. Then the manager decided he wanted to let a minstrel show have the house for a week or two. The Pekin Players protested, but since they did not enjoy the same legal rights as whites, they could not force the manager to honor his contract.

The troupe had to leave New Orleans. They tried another southern city, but after two weeks of losing money daily they knew they could not continue. Those who had the fare back to Chicago went home. The others were forced to stay behind and try to earn return fare. When they tried presenting plays at a tiny theater in a poor black section of town, mobs disrupted the performances and the police did nothing to stop it. It seemed that no one wanted the "Northern Yankee niggers" to succeed.

Eventually, all the stranded Pekin Players managed to make it back to Chicago. They did not attempt a southern tour again! Over the next few years, the troupe provided valuable training for a number of very talented actresses and actors, some of whom would go on to be successful on the stage.

The Lafayette Theatre Stock Players

The Lafayette Theatre, at 2227 Seventh Avenue (corner of 131st Street), was built in 1912 to present white plays to white audiences. But the builders of the two thousand seat theater had misjudged the population shift to Harlem. They soon found themselves with a white theater and a segregated seating policy in an area that was becoming increasingly black.

In the meantime, many blacks were feeling the need for a real black theater in Harlem. One was Lester Walton, a drama critic for the black newspaper New York *Age.* He didn't like the fact that the only image of blacks on the stage was the stereotype. It was time for a black dramatic stock company in Harlem. So, he leased the Lafayette Theatre and set about forming a stock company from among the many able black theater people in the city.

The Lafayette Theatre stock company was packed with talent. Almost everyone in it had been associated with the Cole and Johnson or Williams and Walker shows. Several troupe members had spent time at the Pekin Theatre in Chicago, among them

Charles Gilpin, who would later become famous for his role as the Emperor Jones in Eugene O'Neill's play of the same name. The group presented a great variety of shows. There was a season of grand opera. There were presentations of popular plays like *Dr. Jekyll and Mr. Hyde* and *The Count of Monte Cristo.* In the spring of 1916, during the celebration of the 300th anniversary of William Shakespeare's death, they staged *Othello* starring E. S. Wright and Margaret Brown. Since blacks were not welcome in Broadway theaters, they produced black versions of popular Broadway shows.

The venture was highly successful at first. The popular plays were able to go on tour to black theaters in other cities, like the Howard in Washington and the Dunbar in Philadelphia. One show, *The Darktown Follies,* was particularly successful. Written and staged by an ex-member of the Williams and Walker company, J. Leubrie Hill, it was produced in 1913. The finale to the first act was especially exciting. To the music of a song called "At the Ball," the whole company formed a long chain that snaked around the stage, singing and dancing. The number made headlines even in the downtown white newspapers, and soon whites were flocking to Harlem to see it. Florenz Ziegfeld liked the "At the Ball" number so much that he bought it for inclusion in his own show, and it was one of the greatest hits the Follies ever had.

Two years later the Lafayette troupe tried to repeat the success of *The Darktown Follies* with a similar show. Called *Darkydom,* it had music by Will Marion Cook, starred a popular black comedy team called Miller and Lyles, and brought fame to a young male singer named Opal Cooper.

But the fortunes of the Lafayette were inconstant. As World War I approached, the tastes of Harlem's black theatergoers began to change. At first, local audiences had enjoyed the opportunity to see plays they had been unable to see before, but once they were able to see them many found that they didn't enjoy them. They preferred melodrama and musical comedy, and since a stock company can't last long without an audience, the Lafayette players were forced to narrow their range of offerings. Still, whatever their presentations, black stock companies like the Lafayette's were giving black actors and directors and composers and technicians experience and training they could not otherwise have gotten, and they were giving black audiences the opportunity to see black people on stage in something other than blackface.

The Lafayette players, for example, presented shows in which black men and women actually displayed tender, romantic love toward one another. This was something that could never have been done on a white stage. As the writer James Weldon Johnson explained in his book *Black Manhattan* "One of the well-known taboos was that there should never be any romantic love-making in a Negro play. If anything approaching a love duet was introduced in a musical comedy, it had to be broadly burlesqued. The reason behind this taboo lay in the belief that a love scene between two Negroes could not strike a white audience except as ridiculous. The taboo existed in deference to the superiority stereotype that Negroes cannot be supposed to mate romantically, but do so in some sort of minstrel fashion or in some more primeval manner than white people."

Unfortunately, the context in which these tender love scenes between Negroes were presented was usually a white play. No serious, dramatic plays about black life written by blacks were ever presented by the Lafayette players. As time went on, their offerings were almost entirely musical comedies, because that's what the Harlem audiences wanted. The serious actors began to leave the Lafayette company and go on to other things, and around 1920 the Lafayette Theatre was taken over by new managers, the Coleman Brothers, who concentrated on musical stage shows. It was later taken over by the Schiffman family, who continued the musical stage show fare. The Lafayette dramatic stock company would be reborn decades later at the New Lafayette Theatre, as we shall see.

The Lincoln Theatre Troupe

Scott Joplin found out that black audiences just weren't ready for portrayals of real Negro life when he tried to stage his folk opera *Treemonisha* in New York. Joplin had already made a name for himself as a composer of ragtime, but he wasn't particularly happy about what ragtime had become—a music associated with honky-tonks, saloons and "Tin Pan Alley." He wanted to show that it was a complex and beautiful music, and he had written *Treemonisha* for that purpose. It was the story of a young girl in the South whose parents sacrifice to give her an education and who uses that education to lead her people away from their primitive superstitions. The dream of Joplin's life was to get *Treemonisha* produced, but the Harlem audience that saw its one performance at the Lincoln Theatre, without props or costumes, in 1915 just wasn't ready for such a play. Southern plantations and black superstitions were too much a part of the recent past of many in the audience. They could appreciate the subject matter, but they were not ready to look at their folk past as art.

When *Treemonisha* was staged, the Lincoln Theatre had only recently been converted from a movie house to a place of live entertainment in hopes that it could do as well as the Lafayette. It offered much more variety of entertainment than the Lafayette did: a new four-act play every week, six vaudeville acts which changed semi-weekly, and photoplays that changed every day, not to mention a black orchestra of seven pieces to entertain the audience in between shows.

To present the weekly four-act play, a stock company was established. The first director was Billie Burke, a manager of long experience. Most of the company had gained some experience in vaudeville, but they had to work hard in order to present plays in such rapid succession. Just learning all those lines required tremendous effort. The company did their job well considering their limited experience, particularly the leading man and woman, Walker Thompson and Ophelia Muse. It must be remembered that the troupe was not playing to the easiest audiences who ever sat for a show. In an article in the June 1916 issue of *Theatre* magazine, a white writer describes the Lincoln's audience. Although the writer reveals some typical prejudices, what she wrote was probably correct:

The attitude of the audience gathered in their own theatre—they regard it as such—has little in common with that of the sophisticated playgoer. Dramas, more ambitious than a vaudeville sketch, are a new experience to them, or rather, were a new experience when Mr. Burke staged his intitial production. The response, particularly during the early weeks of the innovation, was emotional and erratic. Even now, with a clientele partially educated in stage effects, Mr. Burke finds that strong bits of melodrama, anything, in fact, that excites fear or horror in the audience, is met by laughter verging on hysteria. The action generally is followed by silence until a striking climax arouses a contagious and noisy demonstration.

Having experimented with drama of many types, the director has discovered a marked preference for productions permitting the use of drawing rooms and pretty clothes. It is always a great point in a play's favor if the actors, and more especially the actresses, are well dressed. The negro is essentially interested in ladies and gentlemen and has scant sympathy for crooks or Western bandits.

Eventually, the Lincoln, like the Lafayette, switched to an all-vaudeville and musical comedy bill. There could be little advancement in black theater, in presenting real black life on the stage, if the audiences did not want to see plays of this type. Still, progress had been made in another important area during the second decade of this century—the musical comedy.

4
Riding the Dream

From Realism to Renaissance, 1917–1921

Black audiences were not alone in preferring musical comedies and melodramas to serious plays. Americans in general in the pre-World War I period did not see the stage as the proper place for realism and naturalism.

Although European drama had long been treating the themes of crime and passion, lust and human limitation, not much drama of this type had been imported to the United States. The main reason for this, according to some historians, is that Americans had a one-sided view of themselves. Americans were supposed to be energetic, hard-working, rugged individuals who loved God and country and who always triumphed in the end. This being the case, there was no room for tragedy, unhappy endings or statements suggesting that people couldn't be perfect if they just tried a little harder. American novelists had begun to introduce realism into their work—Mark Twain among them—and interestingly enough many of their most realistic stories featured blacks. The Negro, being considered less perfect than the white, seemed much better adapted to tragedy and human limitation. When white playwrights began to introduce realism onto the stage, they, too, chose Negro life as their vehicle.

attention was soon taken up by the fighting in Europe. *Three Plays* was moved to the Garrick Theatre, closer to the main theater section, but even major Broadway productions could not keep their audiences in such troubled times and *Three Plays* soon closed.

Although the war put a damper on the large commercial theater, theatrical activity did not completely stop. More white playwrights were experimenting with black themes, still the only vehicles through which anything approaching reality could comfortably be portrayed. These playwrights and their works provided the means by which Charles Gilpin, one of the greatest black actors in history, finally got his big break.

Charles Gilpin

Gilpin was born in Richmond, Virginia, in the early 1870s. He left school at the age of 12 to learn the printing trade. The reason he turned to acting was that his earnings as a printer were not enough. As he told Mary B. Mullett, a writer for *American Magazine,* "My becoming an actor was not due to any dreams of a stage career, but simply because I was trying to earn my bread and butter. I drifted into it because I had taken part in little plays and entertainments at school, where one of the teachers had given me some training in speaking and acting. But as for having an ambition to become a real actor—well, hitching one's wagon to a star is not an attractive pastime for a colored boy. All the stars seem to have 'Keep Off' signs, so far as he is concerned."

Gilpin started out doing song and dance and comedy routines in seedy honky-tonk bars. He then "graduated" to vaudeville. As time went on, he had an urge to do serious dramatic work, but white managers and white audiences didn't think blacks were capable of serious acting. As Gilpin recalled, "Once, when Lillian Morrison and I were doing a turn together in vaudeville, I elaborated a routine and made it a genuine bit of a story.

But the manager said, 'See here! You can't do that! *That's* a sketch!'

"Do you see? We were colored! Therefore, we must not be permitted to *act*. Only white folks were allowed to do that. Apparently, colored folks were not supposed to be regular human beings, with a knowledge of life. They were just human eccentricities, that did certain old tricks, wore certain kinds of queer clothes, and were funny, the way monkeys in a zoo are funny."

Gilpin was intent on doing serious acting. One of the original eleven members of the Pekin Players, he was one of the nine who went on tour to New Orleans, an experience he recalled with great bitterness. He later went to New York and, while holding down regular jobs as an elevator man and a switchboard operator at large apartment houses, was a member, at different times, of the Williams and Walker, Lafayette and Lincoln companies. So he was hardly a newcomer to the stage when John Drinkwater, a British playwright, chose him for the role of the Reverend William Custis in his play, *Abraham Lincoln.*

Drinkwater's play, based largely on a biography of Lincoln written by a British writer, contained a number of errors. The Rev. William Custis, for example, was supposed to represent Frederick Douglass, the black man who had escaped from slavery and become a powerful orator and one of the heros of the northern Abolitionist movement before the Civil War. The English biographer had wrongly described Douglass as "a well-known Negro preacher," and the playwright Drinkwater had carried the error into his play. Worse still, Drinkwater had written all of Rev. Custis's lines in his idea of Negro dialect—which not only was wrong from the standpoint of how Frederick Douglass or even most real black preachers of the time spoke but had nothing in common with black dialect of any sort!

But Gilpin took the part, perhaps because he wanted to be on a stage enough to take any part, perhaps because he saw that, despite the embarrassing dialect, there was considerable potential in the role. In one scene, the Rev. Custis is invited to the White House by President Lincoln for a conference. Their discussion, which touches on black strivings for freedom, is strong and moving, and Gilpin made the most of the opportunity afforded him in this scene. While the play, which opened on December 15, 1919, at the Cort Theatre in New York, received mixed reviews, Gilpin's performance was unanimously praised. Perhaps this was what made Eugene O'Neill choose him for the title role of his play *The Emperor Jones.*

O'Neill was another white American playwright who in his search for a form that he called "supernaturalism" had turned to Negro subjects. Two of his earlier plays had been produced in 1918 and 1919 at the Provincetown Playhouse, a tiny theater in Greenwich Village that had become identified with new faces and new ideas. But *The Emperor Jones* was his most ambitious effort yet to present what he called "the self-defeating self-obsession" that was the twentieth-century human condition.

It is the story of an ambitious, boastful southern black who works as a pullman porter. He kills a man then escapes from jail and flees to a remote jungle island. There, through cleverness and guile, he sets himself up as emperor, complete with palace, ribbon-bedecked uniform, and unlimited power. But he misuses that power and his subjects eventually rise up against him. He escapes into the jungle and is on his way to safety, when all his fears and guilt return to haunt him. In running away from them he runs back into the clutches of his vengeful subjects.

Since the real theme of the play is that man is his own worst enemy and that when the deceptions and tricks that have propped him up are removed he falls victim to his own fears and his own primitive nature, there was no need for O'Neill to make the title character black. But he probably realized that white audiences would be more ready to accept his jungle scenes—when the people the emperor has hurt or mistreated come back to haunt him—if the haunting was done to a black

59

man. After all, didn't the stereotype portray blacks as having a long history of voodoo and still being semiprimitive? With a black man as the central character in what is practically a one-man show, O'Neill needed a powerful black actor. He would not regret choosing Charles Gilpin.

The play and Gilpin—linked together forever in theater history—became famous practically overnight. Critics compared the play to *Othello;* they didn't know to whom to compare Gilpin. There was no one else with that kind of power onstage. As the ill-fated emperor, Gilpin reached the highest point of achievement on the legitimate American stage that had ever been reached by a black.

The awards poured in. He received the Spingarn Medal from the National Association for the Advancement of Colored People (NAACP) that year for "the highest or noblest achievement by an American Negro during the preceding year or years." The same year, 1920, the Drama League named him one of the ten people who had done most for the American theater in the past year. But events associated with that latter award served to remind Gilpin, and other black Americans, that despite all the acclaim, the actor was still a Negro and therefore a second-class citizen.

It was the custom of the Drama League to hold an annual dinner to honor the year's winners. When Gilpin was invited to attend there was a storm of controversy, and great pressure was put on the Drama League to withdraw the invitation. Although some of this pressure came from within the League itself, the committee that had chosen Gilpin and extended the invitation stood firm. The pressurers then turned to Gilpin and tried to get him to stay away from the dinner, but the actor stood firm in his resolve to be there, come what might. In the end, the dinner was held, Gilpin attended, and American life managed to settle back down to business as usual. It seems hard to believe that so much controversy could have been created by a simple dinner invitation. But it was a serious issue then.

Charles Gilpin as he appeared in O'Neill's *Emperor Jones*.
(MUSEUM OF THE CITY OF NEW YORK)

Gilpin remained with *The Emperor Jones* throughout its long and successful run, first downtown and then uptown. He was then faced with the serious question "Where do I go from here?" There were almost no good black roles around. Besides, as Gilpin explained to Mary B. Mullett, "do you know that it is hard for a colored man to get a chance to play even negro parts in regular companies? I played such a part in one company, and some of the actors used to stand outside my dressing-room and talk about me, evidently intending me to overhear them. 'Why did they get a nigger for that part?' they would say. 'A white man could play it better than any nigger that was ever born!' When we arrived in a town, there would be on the call board a list of the members of the company, with the hotels to which they might go. But *my* name was never among them.

I was a pariah dog who must hunt a kennel for himself, if he was to have one."

After *The Emperor Jones* closed, Charles Gilpin went back to running elevators. Over the next eight years he would remain active in the black theater. He would help start a theater company in Cleveland. He would continue to give all he had to the theater until his death on May 6, 1930. That the larger, white theater did not take advantage of his gifts and what he had to give in those last years, and before, is as much that theater's loss as it was his.

It would be many years before black actors and actresses in general would be taken seriously. It would be many years before real-life black drama by blacks would find its way to any but the smallest community theaters. The black audience and the white audience still preferred to see blacks in musical comedy and variety shows, so it is no surprise that these were the kinds of shows presented in most black theaters of the day. Moreover, since the number of black theaters was limited, each was forced to present a wide range of live entertainment geared to all levels of taste. It was not unusual for a black theater to present opera singers, blackface comedians, classically trained dancers, clowns and jugglers, and jazz musicians all in the same evening. The audience members would watch the acts they liked and go out for a smoke or something to eat during the acts they weren't interested in. Admission was usually twenty-five cents, and that included a chance at a door prize, which was usually a ham or a turkey but might be a gold tooth.

Each of the black theaters of any size was on a circuit, which means that the same acts went from one theater to the next. The Keith and TOBA circuits are two examples. The TOBA circuit was the largest. The initials stood for Theatre Owners Booking Agency, but the performers who played this circuit claimed that they really stood for Tough on Black Acts.

Unless you were a headliner, the pay was dreadful. You traveled "second-class" train, playing small towns as well as cities. Costumes and sets were minimal, and performers had to depend on the resident band of each theater for back-up or background music. In a place like New Orleans's Lyric Theatre, the house band was likely to be excellent, but that was not the case in some of the small-town theaters. Life on the circuit was an endless series of one-night stands, cheap hotel rooms, take-out meals, crowded trains and inattentive audiences. It was a life of constant worry about being paid and about not being paid enough even when you were paid, but the peformers on the circuit rarely thought seriously about giving it up. They were true performers. Appearing before an audience—making them laugh, giving them enjoyment—was as important to them as breathing.

Not all black performers were confined to the strictly black circuit. White vaudeville houses booked the better and more popular black acts, but they did so sparingly. They usually billed one black act per show which is why the comedy team of Miller and Lyles and the musical team of Sissle and Blake did not meet sooner, although both teams had been active on the vaudeville circuits for several years. Once the meeting occurred, the four performers went on to create *Shuffle Along,* the show that would bring the Negro back to Broadway.

Shuffle Along

Noble Sissle and Eubie Blake had come together in 1915. Blake had already made a name for himself as a ragtime composer; Sissle had been a singer with several bands. After World War I broke out, Sissle enlisted in the Army and helped form the 39th Infantry Band. When he got out of the Army, he and Blake teamed up again as "The Dixie Duo." They did not perform in blackface—indeed, they were one of the first black acts to play without burnt cork—and they always dressed in the height of elegance. They soon became a very popular act in the white vaudeville houses.

Fluornoy Miller and Aubrey Lyles were a blackface comedy-dancing act who had started out in college theatricals at Fisk University in Nashville, Tennessee. They later played at the Pekin Theatre and went on tour in England before spending several years on the Keith vaudeville circuit.

The two acts happened to come together one summer evening in Philadelphia in 1920. The occasion was an NAACP benefit. The four men got to talking backstage, and before long the conversation turned to the problems of blacks on the stage. All agreed that the only way to put black performers on the white stage with any dignity was through musical comedy, and so they decided to work together to create their own show.

They put the show together very quickly. Basically, it was a combination of their respective acts, organized loosely around a thin plot line—the election for mayor of all-black Jimtown, Mississippi. When they put out casting notices in the theater papers and the black newspapers, black talent from across the country responded, including veterans from the Williams and Walker and Cole and Johnson shows and the Lafayette, Lincoln and Pekin companies.

The foursome now had a show and performers, but they had no money. Miller and Lyles went to Al Mayer, who had once worked for the Keith circuit. He agreed to introduce them to the Cort family, who owned several theaters, including the Cort Theatre. The Cort family was in financial trouble, but they nevertheless offered the use of an old broken-down theater, and leftover sets and costumes from shows that had flopped. The foursome eagerly accepted the offer and began rehearsals at the 63rd Street Theatre for the show they had decided to call *Shuffle Along.*

During the rehearsal period, they filled in the rough outlines of the show, and much of the material they added arose from the props they had on hand. The Corts had given them some slave field, workers costumes, so to integrate them into the show they created a plantation scene and a song called "Bandana

Days." They also had some oriental costumes, so they wrote "Oriental Blues."

In those days it was usual to take a show on an out-of-town tour before bringing it to New York. The four partners knew they must do this, but what would they use for money? Somehow they managed. Eubie Blake, who is ninety-seven years old at this writing, later told Robert Kimball and William Bolcom, authors of *Reminiscing With Sissle and Blake,* "We'd play one-night—if we were lucky, two-night—stands. No one knew us, so they'd only book us for a short time. We'd get good reviews in one town, but before they could do us any good we'd be on to another town—that is, if we had the money. One night Sissle and I were sitting on the steps of a building, and Sissle was writing out checks. They weren't any good until we could wire the box office receipts into the New York bank—we were always one day behind at the very least. I looked up. 'Sissle,' I say, 'do you know where you're sitting?' 'No,' he said, and looked around. We were sitting on the steps of the jailhouse, writing bum checks! We broke up in a fit of laughing and couldn't stop."

By the time the show was ready to open at the 63rd Street Theatre in New York it had an $18,000 deficit. More important, it had an eager and energetic company of talented singers and dancers and musicians plus some wonderful songs like "I'm Just Wild About Harry," "In Honeysuckle Time," and "Gipsy Blues," several of which were to become familiar around the world.

One song in the show called "Love Will Find a Way" was to be sung by a man and a woman in love. Honest, tender, uncomic love between blacks was still considered unacceptable on the white stage. When Jesse Shipp, a veteran of the old Williams and Walker shows, heard that Sissle and Blake had written a song for *Shuffle Along* with the title "Love Will Find A Way," he said "You're crazy" and walked off, shaking his head.

Eubie Blake (playing piano) and Noble Sissle during rehersals for *Shuffle Along.*   (NEW YORK PUBLIC LIBRARY AT LINCOLN CENTER)

According to Kimball and Bolcom, Noble Sissle later said, "On opening night in New York this song had us more worried than anything else in the show. We were afraid that when Lottie Gee and Roger Matthews sang it, we'd be run out of town. Miller, Lyles, and I were standing near the exit door with one foot inside the theater and the other pointed north toward Harlem. We thought of Blake, stuck out there in front, leading the orchestra—his bald head would get the brunt of the tomatoes and rotten eggs. Imagine our amazement when the song was not only beautifully received, but encored. During the intermission we told Blake what we had been doing, and he came near to killing us."

The show was what is called a "sleeper" (an unexpected success). It had arrived quietly in New York and the major critics hadn't bothered to show up on opening night. The reviews by those who did attend, however, were good enough to interest the top critics. When they in turn saw the show, several gave it rave reviews. In no time, *Shuffle Along* was a smash hit.

As musical comedy shows go, *Shuffle Along* was in many ways mediocre. The plot line was thin, and the production was quite amateurish—and no wonder, considering the lack of money and the necessity to adapt the show to sets and costumes discarded from other shows. But the music and dancing were wonderful, and the cast was so eager and full of energy that the spectators couldn't help getting excited. The white audiences couldn't possibly understand what it meant to those talented and hungry black performers to be on the New York white stage in a show entirely written and staged by blacks, in a show that had somehow survived lack of money and all kinds of mishaps on the road. This was what they had worked months for, indeed, what they'd worked all their lives for, and they danced as if their lives depended on it. The audiences could sense the combination of joy and nervous energy that radiated from the stage and it was a wonderful feeling. Alan Dale, the critic for the New York *American,* described the mood inside the theater as follows: "At times it seemed as though nothing would stop the chorus from singing and dancing except ringing down the curtain. They revelled in their work; they simply pulsed with it, and there was no let-up at all. And gradually any tired feeling that you might have been nursing vanished in the sun of their good humor and you didn't mind how long they 'shuffled along.' You even felt like shuffling a bit with them. All of which I admit isn't usual in dear old Forty-second street."

Elsewhere in that review Dale described the show as full of "pep," and it was this "pep" that really attracted audiences. Americans needed a lift in those days. World War I was over by now but its profound effect on the country lingered on. The nation had lost its blind faith in itself and in mankind. There was a cynicism that had not been present before.

This cynicism was expressed mostly by American intellectuals and the urban wealthy. The average man or woman on the street was too busy working and worrying about day-to-day living to spend much time thinking about what the war had been about and what it meant to the national psyche. Those who did have the time to reflect criticized the mass industrialization that had been stimulated by the war. America, they said with great distaste, had entered the "Machine Age," which writer Carl Van Vechten described as the "profound national impulse that drives the hundred millions steadily toward uniformity." A creeping sameness was spreading across the land. Life had become boring.

Shuffle Along showed that innocence and excitement were still alive in the Negro. The black world had all the sensuousness and life rhythm that white America had lost. The intellectuals and the bored socialites "discovered" the Negro through *Shuffle Along*. They saw the show again and again—critic George Jean Nathan saw it five times. The show ran for a full year, and it started a whole new era for blacks on Broadway, as well as a whole new era for blacks in all the creative fields. For *Shuffle Along* is often said to have marked the start of the Harlem Renaissance, a time when Harlem became a playground for whites, and when many black artists and writers received white critical and financial support and were able for the first time to see their works exhibited, their books published and their poetry read.

5
In De Lawd's Pastures

Conflict and Compromise, the 1920s

Black Americans in general were very pleased that the white population had discovered the "New Negro," as he was being called in the 1920s. (Blacks of course knew that there was nothing new about themselves, except that whites were finally paying attention to them). The new focus on Negroes meant that black entertainers were getting work and books by blacks were being published. There was some reason to hope that race relations and conditions for blacks in general would improve as a result. But there were many blacks who recognized that the "New Negro" was merely a jazz-age version of the old plantation darky, a sort of pet rather than a person. Some who recognized the situation for what it was nevertheless accepted white support and this caused them a great deal of conflict. They could either be true to their convictions—refuse to be the white man's pet and find themselves denied the opportunity to publish their books or play their music—or they could compromise their beliefs and enjoy a degree of success in the white world. Most chose to compromise, because they had no other way to see their work come alive. But at the same time they bemoaned their lack of artistic freedom, as did the black intellectuals.

W. E. B. DuBois was one of these intellectuals. A brilliant man and an important black spokesman, he was deeply concerned that American blacks had never produced any truly black drama. He believed that the development of a real black theater was very important for the black self-image. As he saw it, real black dramas would have to conform to four basic principles. They must be: "I. *About us.* That is, they must have plots which reveal Negro life as it is. II. *By us.* That is, they must be written by Negro authors who understand from birth and continual association just what it means to be a Negro today. III. *For us.* That is, the theatre must cater primarily to Negro audiences and be supported and sustained by their entertainment and approval. IV. *Near us.* The theatre must be in a Negro neighborhood near the mass of ordinary Negro people."

Considering that there never had been a real black American theater, DuBois's conditions seemed like a tall order, but he and others were willing to try to meet them. DuBois had become Director of Publicity and Research for the NAACP in 1910 and immediately started a monthly magazine called *Crisis.* Over the years, through the magazine, he launched an ambitious literary and artistic program. In 1924 he added a theater branch onto that program, helping to organize a little-theater group called the Krigwa Players. For a time, the Krigwa Players did very well in finding and presenting plays about blacks that were written, acted, directed and seen by blacks. In 1927, the group presented a play called *A Fool's Errand,* written by a young black New York woman named Eulalie Spence, as their entry in the Little Theatre Tournament.

They didn't win first prize, the David Belasco trophy, but the play received an award as one of the best unpublished manuscript plays in the contest. Unfortunately, it took more than short plays in small theaters for small audiences to establish a living, important black theater. The kinds of serious black dramas the Krigwa Players were trying to present just couldn't compete with the big Broadway musicals that all followed the same basic formula as *Shuffle Along.* As historian Nathan Huggins explained in his book, *Harlem Renaissance:*

The real threat to Negro theater was success. That was, after all, the name of the American game, and it was impossible for people who had always had very little to resist the temptation to make it big. This worked in two ways to undermine efforts to sustain an ethnic theater. First, since plays which were written by Negroes were scarce, it was always a temptation to borrow or adapt white plays. Conditions did not encourage the suffering through on thin or limited material with the hope of forcing the development of playwrights in the long run. Also, the audience would have to be educated into being supporters of such a theater. After all, they were Americans and affected by the good and bad taste of their countrymen. Like other Americans, blacks knew a commercial success—even when they might not know whether or not it was good—and their entertainment was tailored to the standards of mass culture. . . . There was something to be proud of when a black person made it big in any field; the theater was no exception. As long as that was so, it was futile to talk of folk theater. And finally, Negro performers were ultimately pulled into the commercial star system. Success was tangible and important; it was acclaim, and it was money. It is unreasonable, if not unfair, to expect men and women of talent to pass up their "chance" in order to sustain an ethnic theater which was problematic at best.

Although efforts like the Krigwa Players failed after a time, a few serious black dramas written and performed by blacks were produced during the 1920s. In 1925, for example, a play by a black was staged at the Frolic Theatre in New York. Titled *Appearances,* it was noteworthy for its mixed cast of 14 white and three black performers. The playwright, Garland Anderson, was a bellboy and switchboard operator in a San Francisco hotel, and the play first opened in that city. It later played in New York and then went on to London.

In 1929, *Harlem,* a play written by Wallace Thurman in collaboration with William Rapp, was produced. It was about a mother and her children who go to Harlem from the South and who are destroyed by the violence and the vice of the big-city streets. Thurman knew Harlem inside out and, although the play reflected his inexperience as a playwright, it was so powerful and realistic at times that it made the audience squirm. Unfortunately, Thurman was one of the black artists who felt most keenly the conflict between writing what his white patrons wanted and seeing his work produced, or maintaining his artistic freedom and having none of his plays staged. In time the conflict became too much for him. He turned to alcohol and died tragically early.

In spite of a handful of black productions, it was white playwrights who did the most to sustain whatever serious black drama and serious black acting there was throughout the 1920s. Eugene O'Neill had continued writing plays about Negro life, and one of his plays would cause a black actor named Paul Robeson to become the most famous black actor of this century.

Paul Robeson

Paul Robeson was born in Philadelphia, Pennsylvania on April 9, 1898, the son of a Methodist minister. His mother died when he was six years old, and he and his father and brother carried on alone. Paul grew up to be an excellent student and a fine athlete. He was so good at sports that on graduation from high school he was offered a football scholarship to all-white Rutgers University in New Jersey. He later went on to law school at Columbia University, living in Harlem and working at odd jobs in order to pay his tuition.

It was quite by chance that Robeson became an actor. The Harlem branch of the YMCA, to which he belonged, decided in 1920 to put on Ridgely Torrence's *Three Plays for a Negro Theatre*. Paul was asked to play the role of Simon in *Simon the Cyrenian*. Torrence and another white playwright, Eugene O'Neill, and the founders of the Provincetown Playhouse were among those who attended the Harlem Y production. At the time, O'Neill and the Provincetown Players were looking for someone to play the role of Brutus Jones in the O'Neill play *The Emperor Jones*. Impressed with Robeson's sonorous voice and commanding stage presence, they asked him if he would be interested in the part. Robeson read the script and grew furious. He felt that the play portrayed blacks as savages and said as much to O'Neill and the Provincetown Playhouse people. As we have seen, it was Charles Gilpin who eventually played the part of Brutus Jones.

While at law school, Robeson became increasingly attracted to the stage. Two years later he accepted the leading role in a play called *Taboo* by a white female playwright named Mary Hoyt Wyborg. His performance didn't create much excitement in New York—in fact, the critic Alexander Woolcott wrote that Paul Robeson would be best off giving up acting for *any* other career—but he went on tour with the play in England and enjoyed the experience.

Upon receiving his law degree in the spring of 1923, Robeson tried going into practice, but that wasn't an easy thing for a black man to do in the 1920s. All the black businessmen in Harlem had white attorneys, and at the one white law firm where he managed to get a job the white secretaries refused to take dictation from him.

In 1924, the Provincetown Playhouse people contacted Robeson and offered him the lead in not one but two plays by Eugene O'Neill: *All God's Chillun Got Wings* and a revival of *The Emperor Jones*. The salary of $75 a week sounded attractive to Robeson, who was out of work and despondent, and he accepted the offer.

When the Provincetown Players announced in February 1924 that Robeson would play both leads, it created quite a bit of interest in him. The New York *Times* ran a biographical sketch about him, emphasizing his athletic career. But this publicity was nothing compared to the controversy occasioned by the publication of *All God's Chillun Got Wings* in a magazine called *American Mercury* shortly thereafter.

The play was about a young black intellectual named Jim who marries Ella, a white woman. Society's reaction to the marriage is predictable, and drives Ella to prostitution and mental collapse. When the real-life American public read the script in the *American Mercury,* it rose up in arms. The whites were against the play because it was about intermarriage, a subject that was absolutely taboo. The blacks objected to O'Neill's portrayal of Jim, who is supposed to be an intellectual, but is in fact presented as a good-natured sentimental type not very far removed from the stereotyped southern "darky." They also felt the playwright showed prejudice by implying that the only kind of white woman who would marry a Negro was a crazy prostitute. There were intensive efforts to prevent the play from being staged, but the Provincetown Players, including Paul Robeson, stood their ground. Robeson may have had reservations about the play himself, but he needed the money and he needed the job.

On opening night there was real fear that something would happen to disrupt the play, but nothing did. Robeson and Mary Blair, the white actress who played Ella, turned in excellent performances, despite the fact that the play itself was weakened because O'Neill changed its dramatic focus right in the middle. After Ella goes mad, the theme changes from the problem of interracial love in a racist society to the problem of how a sensitive man can live with an insane wife.

Still, the play made Paul Robeson famous. Critics exclaimed over his movements, his expressive features, his resonant voice. He was soon giving concerts of spirituals and black work songs at the Provincetown Playhouse, and he quickly became nearly as famous for his singing as he was for his acting. In fact, O'Neill and the Provincetown director, James Light, added a black spiritual to one of the jungle scenes in *The Emperor Jones.* When that play began its second run, Robeson's importance as an actor increased. In 1925, he went to London with the production, thus becoming the first black American dramatic actor to play on the English stage since Ira Aldridge had played Othello there over a half century earlier.

But here the comparison between Robeson and Aldridge ended. Robeson hadn't had enough stage experience to be considered a trained actor, as he was the first to admit. His real skill was singing, a discipline he preferred. When white critics pronounced him a "natural actor," neither he nor blacks who knew anything about acting were pleased. It was like saying that blacks had natural rhythm or were natural athletes. Whites seemed unable to admit that blacks could work and train hard to be good at what they did.

Paul Robeson's next role was that of a black prizefighter in *Black Boy,* a play by two white writers. He then toured in the musical play *Showboat.* Although neither play did much for his acting reputation, the stage experience he gained made him better prepared to play Othello in London. The play opened in 1930. Robeson now had six years of stage experience. He was also older. He brought a tremendous sensitivity to the role, and London critics raved about his "dignity, simplicity and true passion." Although Robeson would forever after be identified with the character of Brutus Jones—even more so than Gilpin because Robeson also appeared in the film version of the play—his favorite role and the one he felt he played best was that of Othello.

The next time Robeson performed as Shakespeare's tragic hero was thirteen years later. He was now forty-five years old and very experienced. He'd appeared in several motion pictures, a few more plays, and had spent nearly ten years giving concerts all over Europe. Mature and dignified, he brought these qualities to that demanding role in an unforgettable way. His portrayal of Othello in the American Theatre Guild production of the play was not only a high point in his career but also a high point in the history of the American theater. *Othello* opened at

Paul Robeson as he appeared in *Othello*.

the Shubert Theatre on October 19, 1943, and ran until July 1, 1944, playing to packed houses for 296 consecutive performances, a record run for Shakespeare in New York.

After World War II, Americans became terribly afraid of communism and communist influence in the United States.

When Robeson publicly criticized the American government for its treatment of black people, he was suspected by some of wishing to overthrow the government. Although he was neither tried nor convicted of any crime, he was forced to turn over his passport. That meant he could not go abroad to perform or even travel. At the same time, he was blacklisted in the United States and denied the opportunity to perform here as well. Not until 1958 was his passport returned. In later years, Americans tried to make up for forcing Paul Robeson to stop performing for eight years and for falsely accusing him of being a traitor. He was given honors and awards. But it was impossible to make up for what had been done.

Although none achieved the stature of Paul Robeson, several other black actors owe the roles they played and the theatrical experience they gained in the 1920s to white playwrights, who were producing some excellent plays about Negro life. The Provincetown Playhouse was again the scene of one of the best of these productions, Paul Green's *In Abraham's Bosom*, which won a Pulitzer Prize in 1927 for the best original American play representing the educational value and power of the stage. It was the story of a young black farmer who works hard for an education which he hopes to use to help his people find a better life. But whites are hostile to his idea, and even his own people are suspicious of him. Ground down by poverty and frustration, he kills his white half-brother in a fit of madness and is lynched.

The play was a powerful one. James Weldon Johnson wrote that it was closer and truer to actual Negro life and probed it more deeply than any drama of the kind that had yet been produced. The three leading players—Jules Bledsoe as Abraham McCranie, Abbie Mitchell as his mother, and Rose McClendon as his wife—gave powerful performances. Wrote one observer who was quoted by Edith Isaacs in *The Negro in the American Theatre*, "It is difficult to remember scenes in any play that were more compelling than the tragic scenes in which these three players appeared together—all artists, all with long theatre training, all understanding that unity among players which the Russians call 'communion.'" All three actors were seasoned performers who had learned their craft through extensive training—at least as extensive as blacks were allowed. Abbie Mitchell, for example, left a convent in Baltimore to audition for Will Marion Cook's *Clorindy—The Origin of the Cakewalk* in 1898 when she was 14 years old. She later took over the lead in the musical and married Cook. She went on to play leads in many of the Williams and Walker shows and sang operatic roles at the Lafayette Theatre in Harlem. By the time she appeared in *In Abraham's Bosom* she was in her mid-40s, but she would remain on the stage for many more years. In fact, the very next year she would have an important role in a play written by whites that remains the most famous play about black life ever produced.

The play was *Porgy.* It was based on a novel by DuBose Heyward, adapted for the stage by Heyward and his wife, Dorothy, and produced by the Theatre Guild during the 1927-28 season. Set in Catfish Row, the waterfront district of Charleston, South Carolina, it told the story of a man named Porgy who had lost his legs and who loved a girl named Bess. It was well-written, excellently staged, and carried a cast of black characters—sixty-one in all—that would have read like a *Who's Who in Black Theater,* if there had been such a thing. *Porgy* was one of the best plays of the season and one of the great successes of the decade. That first version would run in New York and London for a total of two years. Later, a musical version, with a score by George Gershwin, would become probably the best known play of the century.

Unfortunately, *Porgy,* and the later musical version, *Porgy and Bess,* did not represent a forward step in the portrayal of real black life on the stage. The characters in the play were people whom audiences loved and hated, but they were basically stereo-

(From left to right) Rose McClendon, Frank Wilson, and Evelyn Ellis in a scene from *Porgy*.   (MUSEUM OF THE CITY OF NEW YORK)

types. Serena, played in the original version by Rose McClendon, was the traditional strong southern black woman. Porgy was the traditional likable darky—with a heart of gold but not very bright. The laughable dude stereotype was reflected in Heyward's characterization of Sportin' Life, and the sinister northern city stereotype was reinforced in the character of Crown. Even Bess, the play's heroine, was portrayed as a stereotype—the flighty, weak woman who follows whatever man is wooing her at the moment. A much more realistic play, *The Green Pastures,* was produced two years later, and though it never achieved the commercial success that *Porgy* and then *Porgy and Bess* did, it is considered much more important to black theater history.

Also written by a white man, Marc Connelly, and based on the humorous stories of another white man, Roark Bradford, *The Green Pastures* is about black southern religion. In one amusing scene, for example, black angels hold a fish fry in heaven. Despite its humor, Connelly's play has a very serious message—that man has a unique and wonderful relationship with God (called "De Lawd" in the play). *The Green Pastures* was produced at a time when the country as a whole seemed to be turning more to religion. This was the perfect moment for a production about the simple and unquestioning trust of a people in their God.

Connelly's play, which won a Pulitzer Prize, was beautifully performed by a fine cast of actors and actresses. Just about every seasoned black performer was part of its huge cast. But the most talked-about role, that of De Lawd, was held not by a veteran but by a novice—at least on the professional stage. Richard Harrison's only previous theatrical experience had been as a dramatic reader of Shakespeare in black clubs, schools, and churches. He actually had to study the black dialect (in which De Lawd's lines are written) with a *white* coach! Harrison was sixty-five years old when he was signed to the role, but he never missed one of the play's 1,568 straight performances. He even played through a bitter strike called by most of the cast in Washington, D.C., when they learned that the National Theatre there did not admit blacks.

The Green Pastures was later made into a movie, and it is still one of the best known of American plays. Like *Porgy,* it relied very heavily on black stereotypes, but unlike *Porgy* it managed, through the talent and sensitivity of its actors, to cut across racial lines. In the end, *The Green Pastures* was not about black religion but about man and God.

Although the serious plays about blacks that were staged in major theaters during the 1920s were written by whites, that does not mean there were no working black playwrights in this period. No chapter on black theater in the 1920s can be complete without including the work of at least one of them, Willis Richardson, the first black playwright to have a serious black play produced on Broadway and one of the most prolific playwrights in the history of black theater.

Willis Richardson

Richardson was born in Wilmington, North Carolina, on November 5, 1889. After a race riot in Wilmington in 1898, his parents decided to move to Washington, D.C. One of his high school English teachers, Mary Burrill, was a playwright and she encouraged his early interest in drama. Upon graduation in 1910, Richardson became a clerk in the U.S. Bureau of Printing and Engraving, where he remained for forty-five years.

In 1916, Richardson attended a performance of Angelina Grimke's *Rachel,* a play about black life that concentrated on how whites mistreated blacks. As he wrote in *Crisis* magazine in 1919, Richardson sensed the need for "another kind of play; the kind that shows the soul of a people; and the soul of this people is truly worth showing." He began submitting what he felt to be such plays, written for both adults and children, to *Crisis,* the magazine of the NAACP that W. E. B. DuBois edited. Between 1920 and 1921, four of his plays for children were published in *The Brownies' Book,* another NAACP publication, also edited by DuBois. His first adult one-act play, *The Deacon's Awakening,* was published in *Crisis* late in 1920.

Richardson's first break came in 1922, when the newly organized Ethiopian Art Players in Chicago asked W. E. B. DuBois to recommend some black playwrights. DuBois put them in touch with Richardson, and at the end of January 1923 the group presented his one-act play *The Chip Woman's Fortune.*

The play is about a store porter in a small southern town

who is going to lose his job because he hasn't kept up the payments on a record player. Desperate for money, he decides to rob an old woman who rooms with his family. Although she appears to have nothing but what she makes selling coal and wood chips she finds in the street, the man decides she has a fortune hidden away somewhere. She has in fact saved some money which she plans to give to her son who has just been released from prison. The story ends happily. The returning son is so grateful to the porter and his family for taking care of his mother that he gives the porter the money he needs.

The play was so well received during its limited run that it went on tour, opening in Washington, D.C., in April and at the Lafayette Theatre in Harlem in May. It then went to the Frazee Theatre on Broadway.

It was only a one-act play, and it only played Broadway for a week, but it was still a break-through of sorts for the black in the theater, and it helped Richardson get more of his plays produced. His one-act *Mortgaged* was staged at Howard University in March 1924. Except for an earlier production of a play by one of Howard's students, it was the first play by a black playwright ever to be presented at this college for blacks. The Gilpin Players at the Karamu Theatre in Cleveland presented Richardson's *Compromise* in 1925, and in the same year his *The Broken Banjo,* which was produced by the Krigwa Players in New York, won first prize in the *Crisis* awards. Other one-act plays of his were presented by various theater groups in the 1920s, and several of his one-act plays were included in drama anthologies during those years, but none except *The Chip Woman's Fortune* made it to Broadway.

Richardson also wrote six three-act plays, but they were never produced or published. Those who know about Richardson and have read his plays believe that his work as a whole never got the acclaim that it deserved because this pioneering twentieth-century black playwright was ahead of his time. Perhaps someday he will receive the attention he should.

6
"Double, Double Toil and Trouble"

The Depression Years and the FTP, the 1930s

The stock market crash of October 1929 plunged America into a deep and long-lasting depression. Banks closed, businesses were ruined and people lost their jobs and savings. The newspapers were filled with headlines about men jumping from windows because they were financially ruined. As average income per person tumbled from $681 in 1929 to $495 in 1933 and unemployment shot up from six million in January 1931 to 15 million by the end of 1932, middle-class people stopped buying clothes and household items, gave up their telephones, and even started making their own soap at home. The poor, who had less to begin with, began going without meat, coffee, tea, sugar and toilet paper. Sometimes, they had to give up their homes.

Black people as a group were hardest hit by the Depression. As the "last hired and first fired," more lost their jobs than whites did. Since as a group they had always had a hard time making a living, they did not have much in the way of financial reserves—like property, expensive jewelry or money in the mattress—to tide them over. By 1933 there were two million blacks receiving relief—twice as many as there should have been in terms of their percentage of the national population. In the South, where certain menial jobs had traditionally been reserved for blacks—street cleaning, garbage collecting, ditch-digging—the black workers were fired and the jobs given to whites. Without even menial jobs available, many blacks went to the northern industrial cities looking for work, swelling the black population of some of these cities by as much as 25 percent.

If black people were the group that suffered most during the Depression, the theater was the cultural field that had the greatest trouble surviving. The professional stage had been in trouble even before the stock market crash, partly because of the changing times, but mostly because of short-sightedness of those who held power in the theater.

By the late 1920s both movies and radio were seriously threatening the commercial stage, and the theater was not doing much to defend itself. Refusing to take account of the fact that there was more to America than the East Coast, and especially New York City, producers and directors and even actors had made little attempt to take theater away from its traditional centers. Also, although America had developed its own culture, most people with any power in the theater had continued presenting European plays aimed at rich, aristocratic audiences who looked more to Europe than to their own country for "art." When the Depression came and the uppercrust theater patrons lost their money, the theater was in deep trouble. It was difficult to get people on extremely tight budgets to go to a play with tickets averaging around $2.25 per person when the cost of attending a movie was only 25¢ a head! As the Depression deepened, more and more theaters converted into movie houses.

An idea of how bad things were is shown by the fact that two-thirds of Manhattan's playhouses were shut in 1931, putting hundreds of writers, directors, set designers, prop and lighting men, and orchestra members out of work. In the winter of 1931, *Variety,* the theatrical trade journal, reported that there were 25,000 unemployed theatrical people in all phases of the profession. It also found that 3,000 of these people were black, a figure representing nearly all the blacks in the theatrical profession at the time.

But just because the commercial theater went into a slump didn't mean that theater as an art form was dying. On the contrary, during the early 1930s amateur theaters were enjoying a period of growth. Many of the unemployed theater people turned to the "little theaters" (soon to be called community theaters) in cities and towns across the country. Others formed their own touring troupes. The plays they presented were different from the plays they had acted in before the Great Depression began. The Depression caused a lot of resentment against big business, which didn't seem to be suffering nearly as much as the average person. It also threw into stark relief many social and cultural problems that hadn't seemed as evident in more prosperous times. The new theater companies thought it was about time plays started reflecting reality. In New York, a group of professionals and amateurs formed the Theatre Union to "produce plays that deal boldly with the deep-going social conflicts, the economic, emotional and cultural problems that confront the majority of the people."

With so many people unemployed, labor unions increased their membership greatly during the Depression. Labor theater groups sprang up, and were so popular that in 1932 they were able to hold a national conference and to create The League of Workers' Theatres. Other amateur groups formed associations like the Theatre Union in New York. Most of these groups had the same stated aim as the Theatre Union. They presented plays about labor strikes, about poverty and about all the social and economic ills of American society. These kinds of plays came to be called agitation-propaganda plays, agit-prop for short.

Black theater people, amateur or professional, didn't have much to do with this movement. Since they weren't allowed into most labor unions, they weren't part of the labor theater groups. And since there wasn't much integration in the amateur theater they were not well represented in the larger associations that were formed by these groups. Besides, the small black theater groups were more conservative about the kinds of plays they staged. While the white radicals were presenting agit-prop, the black little theater or community theater groups, which were largely middle class, and the black college theaters were still presenting mostly Shakespeare and Greek classics and "safe" plays by well-known white playwrights. In fact, the only "courageous" play written by a black in the early 1930s was *Mulatto* by Langston Hughes.

Langston Hughes

Langston Hughes was born in Joplin, Missouri, on February 1, 1902. When he was very young, his parents separated, causing Hughes to follow his mother from place to place as she looked for jobs. Hughes started writing poetry in high school and, determined to learn more about literature and writing, put himself through Lincoln University, a black college in Pennsylvania.

The Harlem Renaissance began while Hughes was at Lincoln, and he traveled north to New York City as often as he could to be around other black writers. On one of these trips, he met an elderly, wealthy white woman who offered to pay his expenses so he could devote more time to writing. With her support, he wrote more poems and started work on a novel. He was also interested in black theater, and the fall after his graduation from Lincoln he spent several weeks in New York working with a little theater group in Harlem and writing a play called *Mulatto* with his friend and fellow writer, Zora Neale Hurston. It was good enough to interest a producer, who wanted to cast Rose McClendon in one of the leading roles. But the actress got an offer to appear in a Broadway play, and the project was dropped. A disappointed Hughes turned the play over to his New York literary agent and went back to writing poems and novels.

When the Depression came, and Hughes saw the long bread lines and the thousands of blacks out of work, it became harder and harder for him to accept the support of his rich patroness. It also became harder for him to write the kinds of things she wanted him to write. Finally he was forced to tell her that he could no longer accept her support. That was the end of the Harlem Renaissance for Langston Hughes! In fact, the renaissance was also ending at about the same time for most of the other writers and artists who had, very briefly, enjoyed the attention of wealthy and intellectual whites. Langston Hughes later wrote in his autobiography, *The Big Sea*: "I was there. I had a swell time while [the renaissance] lasted. But I thought it wouldn't last long. . . . For how could a large and enthusiastic number of people be crazy about Negroes forever?"

In the spring of 1932, Hughes was invited to accompany a black, Harlem-based motion picture group to Russia, where they planned to make a film on United States race and labor relations. He eagerly accepted the offer. But when the group got to the USSR, they found that the script, written by a Russian who had never been to America, was so full of errors that none of the black actors would agree to act in it. Hughes did get something out of his trip to Russia, however. During his travels around the country, he saw a number of plays and learned a great deal about theater there. Many Russian plays were presented in theaters-in-the-round, with the audience seated around a central stage. There was no scenery to speak of and few props; the performance depended very much on the power of the actors. It occurred to Hughes that this kind of staging might work very well in American black little theater, and he stored the details of the Russian productions in the back of his mind for future use.

Hughes returned to New York in the fall of 1934. Almost as soon as he stepped out of the subway station in Harlem, he ran into a friend who asked if he was in New York to attend rehearsals of *Mulatto*. Hughes had no idea that after five years the play had finally been sold and that Zora Hurston was claiming sole authorship. Several changes had been made to make *Mulatto* more "box office." He didn't approve of them. He also resented the fact that neither he nor any of the black actors were invited to the white producer's opening-night party.

Mulatto ran for a year on Broadway. It then toured the country for two years more, setting a record in America for number of performances of a play written by a black. *Mulatto* was practically the only play written by a black playwright known to the commercial theater, and Hughes had a hard time collecting royalties and keeping authorship of his own play.

Back in Cleveland, where he was forced to return because of his mother's illness, Hughes became involved in a settlement house called Karamu House, from the Swahili word that means both "community center" and "place of enjoyment." A couple named Russell and Rowena Jelliffe had started a small theater company there. The actor Charles Gilpin had been urging the group for some time to present dramas about real black life, and the Karamu people had agreed. Renaming the company the Gilpin Players, they began eagerly looking around for real-life black dramas written by black playwrights. Langston Hughes had clearly come to the right place!

Up to the mid-1930s, the Broadway theater had produced exactly seven plays by black writers, of which *Mulatto* was the last. Clearly, the Gilpin Players of Karamu House in Cleveland were not the only group in the country in need of black input. In 1935, a new publication called *New Theater* magazine announced a national contest for the best play about black life. Many plays were submitted, but only the one sent in by Hughes was thought worthy of production by the judges. Hughes's entry, *Angelo Herndon Jones,* won first prize even though the editors of the magazine considered it dramatically weak.

Hughes took the editors' criticism in stride. After all, he wasn't very experienced at writing plays. But he was eager to learn, and he had a whole company of actors waiting to stage his plays. Indeed, between 1936 and 1937, Karamu House staged six of them. Unfortunately, the Cleveland black community— or at least those who were interested and could afford to buy tickets—was not as forward-looking as Karamu House and the Gilpin Players. Like the Lincoln Theatre audiences in Harlem back in the late teens and early twenties, they were interested in light entertainment, not Hughes's stark presentations of black life. Primarily people newly arrived in the middle class and struggling to hold on to that status in the midst of the worst depression the country had ever been through, they did not want to be reminded of their difficult past.

The experiences of Langston Hughes and the Gilpin Players pretty much summed up the state of the black theater in the early to mid-1930s. It was kind of a Catch-22 situation. Black theater groups who wanted to stage more realistic plays couldn't find the plays to perform. Black playwrights who wanted to write realistic black plays didn't have the experience or the training to do so. When, against great odds, a forward-looking company and a forward-looking, somewhat experienced playwright got together and actually produced realistic plays, the audience that could afford to go to the theater didn't want to see them. Fortunately, help came from the WPA Federal Theatre Project.

As the Depression wore on, President Franklin Delano Roosevelt decided that something had to be done about the massive unemployment in the country, so he started a huge program to put people to work. One of the biggest agencies to be established under this program was the Works Progress Administration (WPA), which was designed to give dignity to the jobless by creating paying jobs. WPA programs ranged from ditch-digging and stone masonry to work in the cultural fields. Unemployed writers wrote manuals and conducted studies, unemployed painters created murals for public buildings, unemployed sculptors fashioned statues for public parks, and unemployed theatrical people created and presented plays. The WPA not only helped the economy by pumping in money in the form of workers' salaries, it also helped bring beauty to the cities and towns of America, and in some instances helped change our nation's cultural life. Nowhere was this more true than in the area of the American theater.

The WPA theatrical program was called the Federal Theatre Project. Its stated purpose was not only to provide work for unemployed theater people, but also to do something the private commercial theater had never done—to bring serious drama to the masses. That meant setting up theaters throughout the nation that would present plays about the daily lives of average Americans, including blacks. The Federal Theatre Project proved to be one of the most important developments in the history of black American theater.

Much of the program's success was due to its project director, Hallie Flanagan. President Roosevelt and WPA director Harry Hopkins had been pressured to appoint a director with experience in the commercial theater. But they wanted someone who loved theater for its own sake rather than the money it made and who would be as excited about setting up a theater in Denver or Chicago as in New York.

Flanagan, who had been active in the noncommercial theater and who had a "national perspective," accepted the controversial appointment immediately and wasted no time in stating her commitment: "While our immediate aim is to put to work thousands of theatre people, our more far-reaching purpose is to organize and support theatrical enterprises so excellent in quality and low in cost and so vital to the communities involved that they will be able to continue after federal support is withdrawn." She then started holding organizational meetings to which she invited respected representatives of all facets of the theater. One of those invited was the actress Rose McClendon.

Since 1926, when she had come to public attention with her

Hallie Flanagan.   (GEORGE MASON UNIVERSITY)

role in *Deep River,* there had been few important plays about
black life staged in New York that had not included McClendon
in the cast. Active in supporting community theater, she was
in the process of organizing a group called the Negro People's
Theatre in Harlem when she was invited to take part in the
organizing of the FTP.

One of Rose McClendon's major suggestions was that there ought to be separate black theater units in the FTP. The project's national leadership agreed. In fact, it was decided that not just blacks but other ethnic groups should have their own units. Another important decision affecting blacks was made at these organizational meetings. It was decided that there would be no segregated seating in any theater that was part of the FTP, nor would any FTP traveling company have segregated traveling accommodations. These were radical decisions for the mid-1930s.

Once a broad organizational outline for the FTP had been set up, the national directorship went to work appointing local directors and setting up the companies and theaters it had been charged with establishing. The range of Negro theater projects alone will give an idea of the scope of the $46 million project. There were two black theater units in New York City alone, and by the time the FTP program was in full operation there were black units in Buffalo, New York; Hartford, Connecticut; Newark and Camden, New Jersey; and Philadelphia, Pennsylvania. And that was just on the East Coast. In the South there were units in Durham, North Carolina; Raleigh, South Carolina; Atlanta, Georgia; Birmingham, Alabama; and New Orleans, Louisiana. In the Midwest, there were black units in Cleveland, Ohio; Detroit, Michigan; and Chicago and Peoria, Illinois. In the West, San Francisco and Los Angeles, California; Portland, Oregon; Seattle, Washington; and the little town of Okmulgee, Oklahoma, had units—making a total of twenty-two cities in all. Never before had blacks been allowed such visibility on the American cultural scene.

The blacks involved in the organization of the FTP were determined that the black theater community should make the most of this opportunity to be seen and heard. They were concerned that, although there was a pool of experienced actors and actresses to call on, there was a serious lack of black playwrights, directors, producers, and stage managers. This was not surprising since all but a few black people active in these fields had been forced to spend much of their time working at other jobs in order to make ends meet. Here was their big chance and they weren't ready.

Rose McClendon felt that the best way for blacks to learn the theater skills they needed was under the direction of someone who already had them. She therefore fought against Hallie Flanagan's proposal to name a black to head up the Harlem unit, insisting that it would be better to have a white director and other white administrators at first. It was to be understood, of course, that an important part of the administrators' duties would be to train blacks to replace them as quickly as possible. The other black representatives at the meetings agreed with Rose McClendon. Still, there was much pressure for black participation on the administrative level. At length, McClendon agreed to share the directorial duties of the Harlem unit, choosing the Englishman John Houseman as her codirector. (Houseman is known to audiences today as the grumpy law professor in both the movie *The Paper Chase* and the television series that was based on it.) White directors or codirectors were also named to most other black units across the country.

Throughout the project's existence, Hallie Flanagan worked closely with her black advisers, asking for and respecting their opinions. Once, for example, the Newark black unit was planning to present Octavus Roy Cohen's play *Come Seven.* The story revolves around a black man who pawns his wife's diamond ring. A number of other blacks in the play seem to spend most of their time stealing chickens and gambling. When the leaders of various national black organizations heard about the play and its plot, they protested to the FTP's National Play Bureau. The ridiculous Negro stereotypes that filled Cohen's play were no better than the insulting images of blacks presented on Broadway, they insisted. The FTP's national leadership agreed, and the play was never produced. In fact, the FTP went on to seek the help of these same black organizations in compiling a library of acceptable plays, works that portrayed blacks as normal human beings.

One of the nicest things about the FTP was that, since it wasn't primarily a profit-making operation, it was in no rush to get a play onto the stage and ticket money into the cashier's box. The national leadership of the FTP insisted on long rehearsals. This gave the playwrights and performers time to smooth out rough spots. It also gave the directors, lighting technicians, and all the other people involved in the staging time to learn more about the total theater environment and the many jobs that were part of a theatrical production. Black seamstresses, for example, got excellent training in these black theater units, acquiring skills that they could continue to use whether they remained in the theater or not; playwrights had the invaluable experience of seeing their work performed; actors and actresses were freed from the limiting character parts—maids and butlers and prostitutes and gamblers and no-accounts of one sort or another in which they had been trapped—and allowed to play complete human beings: people who cried as well as laughed, were victors as well as victims, hoped and worked and loved just like everybody else. Directors had their first chance to direct, and many many others were able for the first time to work on a serious black play. It was an exciting time for them all, and the plays they produced together reflected that excitement.

The Harlem Unit

Of the four units of the Federal Theatre Project set up in New York in 1935, two were black. The primary unit was the Federal Negro Theatre. The second, the Negro Youth Theatre, was designed to develop inexperienced and lesser-known talents. Both were housed in the Lafayette Theatre.

When Rose McClendon died in 1936 at the age of fifty-one, John Houseman carried on the directorial duties of the Harlem unit alone. One of its first major productions was a black version of *Macbeth*. The black actors and actressess of the Harlem unit wanted to prove that they could perform the classics as well as portray servants, but this would be no ordinary version of Shakespeare's play.

Macbeth is about a power-mad Scottish nobleman who murders the king of Scotland with the help of his wife. He is urged to commit the crime by a group of witches who prepare mysterious potions and chant, "Double, double toil and trouble, fire burn and cauldron bubble!" Because Houseman wanted an experienced director with a flair for the dramatic to stage this exciting play, he hired a young white man named Orson Welles, who had just wound up a tour of Shakespeare's *Romeo and Juliet.*

It was unanimously decided to change the locale of the play from Scotland to Haiti. Haiti, famous for its "voodoo" and witchcraft, made a much more exciting setting than Scotland and allowed the black-magic theme of the drama to be played to the hilt.

When Welles discovered a touring African dance group stranded in New York for lack of return passage, he immediately signed them up. He also hired a practicing African witch doctor whom he had somehow found in New York. The musical score for the show was full of voodoo drums and witches' cries, and the jungle sets were exotic and eerie. All the roles were played by blacks: Jack Carter and Edna Thomas were Lord and Lady Macbeth, Canada Lee played Banquo, and Eric Burroughs played the evil Hecate.

The show was a tremendous success. Drama critic Brooks Atkinson praised the Haitian setting as follows in his review of the production: "The witches have always worried the life out of the polite tragic stage. . . . But ship the witches down to the rank and fever-stricken jungle of Haiti, dress them in fantastic costumes, crowd the stage with mad and gabbing throngs of evil worshippers, beat the jungle drums, raise the voices until the jungle echoes, stuff a gleaming, naked witch

Opening night crowd for *Macbeth.*   (GEORGE MASON UNIVERSITY)

doctor into the cauldron, hold up Negro masks in baleful light—
and there you have a witches' scene that is logical and stunning
and a triumph of theatre art.''

After a seven-month run in New York, *Macbeth* went on a
nationwide tour. It not only helped to establish the Harlem
unit of the FTP as an exciting and creative group, but also
gave other black units across the country the courage to do
adaptations of other previously "all-white" plays. And it opened
the range of Shakespeare to blacks; *Othello* would no longer
be the only Shakespearean play they dared to perform.

The Harlem and other black units also used the opportunity
provided them by the FTP to produce plays about the importance of blacks in history. This was quite a forward-looking
step in the 1930s. Nowadays blacks, and whites, are likely to
know quite a lot about black history, thanks to published books
on the subject, television shows and series like "Roots," and
courses taught in most schools, at least during Black History

A scene from *Black Empire*.　　　(GEORGE MASON UNIVERSITY)

Week. But back in the 1930s things were very different. Black history was ignored as if it didn't exist. The black units of the FTP decided to use theater as a way to acquaint blacks with their dramatic past. For 55¢ a ticket, audience after audience would be given an opportunity to learn about the powerful and important roles blacks had played on the stage of history. Black units across the country presented plays about John Henry, the legendary "steel-driving" railroad man, about Booker T. Washington, about African history, and about the black rebellion against France in Haiti in the early 1800s. In fact, two different plays about the revolution in Haiti were produced. One was called *Black Empire* and the other was simply called *Haiti*.

Haiti, first produced by the Harlem unit, was written by a southern white man named William DuBois. In its original form the script had concentrated on the evils of intermarriage and interracial sexual relationships, hardly a pro-black theme. But the Lafayette Theatre's director, Maurice Clark, saw the potential power and drama in the play and felt that with rewriting it could be made to stress the struggle by black Haitians for pride and self-determination.

The two most important black leaders in the Haitian revolution were Toussaint L'Ouverture and General Henri Christophe. *Haiti* is about how a young woman, Odette Boucher, who thinks she is French, finds out from Christophe that she is in fact the daughter of a black man, one of L'Ouverture's aides. In the midst of the rebellion, she must choose between her French upbringing and her black heritage. Odette decides to side with her father and the other Haitian rebels, and she survives the rebellion.

Rex Ingraham played Henri Christophe in the Lafayette Theatre production. A giant of a man, he brought great power to the role. Odette Boucher's father was sensitively portrayed by Alvin Childress, who received considerable acclaim for his portrayal. (Childress went on to play the role of Amos in the radio show "Amos 'n Andy" in the 1940s.) Leonard de Paur, who today holds an important post at Lincoln Center, was the musical director for the show; Bryan Webb was the technical director; and Perry Watkins, who later became the first black man ever admitted to the Set Designer's Union, did the sets. (Another Lafayette Theatre employee, stagehand Henry Kinnard, also got into a union through his work with the FTP. He works for NBC today.)

What did William DuBois think of all this? He'd agreed to most of the changes director Maurice Clark had made because he had wanted very much to see his play produced. But there was one thing he insisted on. John J. O'Connor and Lorraine Brown include in their history of the FTP an anecdote told by Clark: DuBois said, "Listen now, Clark, listen, I've given in to you on every single thing but I want to tell you one thing right here and now that I demand, and that is that on that stage no white hands and no black hands shall touch."

Clark was forced to agree to DuBois's demand in order to put on the play. But he managed to have the last word. As Clark explained later, "the encore was mine. When the curtain came up for the encore, the whites were among the blacks, holding hands, and that's how they took their bows."

Some 77,000 people saw *Haiti* in its Lafayette Theatre run in the spring and summer of 1938. It later played for a week in Boston and was staged by the Hartford black unit as well.

Another important play staged by the Lafayette Theatre unit was George Bernard Shaw's *Androcles and the Lion.* Shaw generously released all of his plays to the Federal Theatre Project. Unlike Eugene O'Neill, who resented blacks presenting his plays, he was eager to see his plays performed by all-black casts. The great Irish dramatist wrote to Hallie Flanagan that "Negroes act with a delicacy and sweetness that make white actors look like a gang of roughnecks."

Shaw's play is about an early Christian named Androcles who removes a burr from a lion's paw. The lion is able to repay this kindness when Androcles and other Christians are thrown to him by the Romans to eat. Arthur "Dooley" Wilson played Androcles, and Add Bates was the lion. Watkins, de Paur and Webb, the same technicians who had worked on *Haiti,* again combined talents in the staging of the Shaw play. With musical substitutions like gospel songs for the hymns in the original play, the Lafayette's production, though true in all important aspects to Shaw's ideas, was uniquely black. It ran for 104 performances.

Still another big FTP hit was *Big Blow,* written by a white man, Theodore Pratt, and produced by the Lafayette Company in November 1938. It concerns a young Nebraska farmer named Wade who moves to Florida for his mother's health and who finds himself pitted against a variety of evil forces in the South. His neighbors distrust him and insects and thieves destroy his crops. When Clay, a black servant, tries to stop a bully from raping a poor orphan girl, Wade comes to the man's defense.

As a mob prepares to lynch both Clay and Wade, a hurricane hits and practically levels the area. Miraculously, Wade's house is left untouched, and the people see that as a sign from God. Wade is accepted at last by his neighbors.

In the New York production, Amelia Romano played the fifteen-year-old orphan girl and Doe Doe Green played Clay. After Clay has saved her from rape by hitting her attacker and is about to be attacked himself by a white mob, the girl tries to protect him. O'Connor and Brown include in their history of the FTP that Amelia Romano recalled years later, "I ran to him and threw my arms around him. Now that embrace got a lot of flak, although Dodie was delighted; a lot of his friends, an awful lot of blacks, came to the theatre for the first time because of [that scene]. There were occasional hisses from the audience, but I refused to change it, because it seemed . . . right to me." In the 1930s it was daring indeed for a white female character to embrace a black male character—even one who had just saved her from a horrible fate.

Big Blow was produced in 1939 in Chicago, Boston and Los Angeles. But because it was anti-southern it never was staged in the South.

In the four years it was in operation, the Harlem unit of the FTP would stage more than twenty other plays, and as the years wore on more and more of the responsibility for directing, scoring, set designing and writing would be taken on by blacks. Eventually, John Houseman and Orson Welles left to start the famous Mercury Theatre. Black men including Carlton Moss, Augustus Smith and Harry Edward replaced them. Moss had been with the unit from the beginning, charged with attracting the black community to the Lafayette Theatre's productions. For the opening night of *Macbeth* he had had huge footprints painted on the sidewalk and arranged for a big brass band to lead the people to the theater. Throughout the life of the project he visited churches and lodge halls to win the community audience. Augustus Smith helped write one of the plays the unit produced—*Turpentine,* about the plight of black workers in the Florida pine woods. Harry Edward held the important post of theater administrator.

Another important black unit was the one in Los Angeles, although it didn't produce anything original for its first few years. Anxious to do more than repeat productions that had originated in other cities, the unit members finally found a good play of their own to stage: *Run, Little Chillun.* The play had been written by Hall Johnson and produced in New York in 1933. Johnson, who had recently left the Harlem unit as musical director, happened to be in Los Angeles and agreed to help with the play. And Clarence Muse agreed to join the unit as *Run, Little Chillun*'s guest director.

Muse was one of the few blacks who had established himself as a director before the beginning of the FTP. He had graduated from Dickinson University with a degree in law, but had made the stage his career instead. A singer and actor, he had performed in over two hundred plays and films, written plays and formed his own theater companies in New York and in the South. Muse would have a long show business career after his work with the FTP. He wrote a number of popular songs, including "When It's Sleepy Time Down South," (Louis Armstrong's theme song), appeared in *Huckleberry Finn* and *Porgy and Bess,* and in the 1970s was still going strong. His film roles included the prophet in the movie "Buck and the Preacher" and the shoeshine man in the movie "Car Wash." With the help of Muse and Johnson and a number of other talented people, the Los Angeles unit went to work staging what was to become one of the most popular FTP productions.

Run, Little Chillun is about the conflict between Christianity and more primitive religion. A man named Jim must choose between the Hope Baptists and the New Day Pilgrims and between two women, the Baptist Ella and the siren Sulamai.

101

The play calls for a large cast, a great deal of music, and lots of storefront church scenes and woodland pagan ceremonies, and everyone involved in the Los Angeles production had a wonderful time. A huge drum eight feet tall and six feet wide was built for the frightening thunder storms that were part of the pagan rites; its thunder sounds shook the theater rafters. A gigantic tree was designed as the setting for the New Day Pilgrim's woodland rituals. One hundred and sixty-five people danced around and between the huge roots rising up out of the ground.

The production was a smash hit in Los Angeles. Tickets were just 55¢, but they were in such demand that "scalpers" (people who buy tickets to hit performances and sell them at a profit to people who will pay almost any price for them) were getting $3 and $4 apiece. The play made enough money to pay for new equipment, sets and costumes for all the Los Angeles units, white and black. And just as important, it gave the Los Angeles black unit a real sense of pride and accomplishment.

Another West Coast black unit, in Seattle, Washington, distinguished itself in the four years of its existence. One of its best-known productions was an adaptation of a play by the ancient Greek playwright Aristophanes—*Lysistrata.* The reason for the production's fame was that it was forced to close after opening night (the wife of the state WPA director decided it was "obscene"). In 1936 the Seattle unit staged *Stevedore,* a play about a strong, determined black dock worker who stands up to the white bosses and unites black and white workers behind him. A powerful play, powerfully acted by the members of the Seattle black unit, it served to put that unit on the map.

The director of the Boston unit heard about the Seattle production of *Stevedore* and decided that his unit should stage the play, too. Ralf Coleman, one of the few black directors of a black unit right from the start, was very much like the hero of *Stevedore*—strong, courageous, and determined. When Federal Theatre Project officials objected to his unit's doing the

The barricade scene from *Stevedore*.

play (they thought the idea of black and white workers uniting smacked of communism), Coleman decided that the members would rehearse on their own time and perform the play in a non-FTP theater in Boston. When the FTP officials learned of his plan, they deliberately scheduled a Federal Theatre performance for the black unit the same night as the opening of *Stevedore* about thirty miles away in Salem, Massachusetts. Coleman got around that problem. He arranged for the performance in Salem to begin earlier and scheduled the performance of *Stevedore* in Boston later. The cast performed in Salem without an intermission, then rushed back to Boston to put on *Stevedore*. The production was excellent, but both cast and audience enjoyed it all the more because the FTP officials had been outsmarted.

In spite of the enterprise of people like Coleman and the efforts of Hallie Flanagan to give the units free rein in their choice of productions, there was quite a bit of censorship in the FTP. The Chicago black unit felt this censorship when it tried to stage one of its first productions, Paul Green's *Hymn to the Rising Son*. The play, which was about prison chain gangs, was declared obscene, although it had already been performed by a regular white theater group in Chicago and had even won a play contest. On opening night of the FTP production, three hundred angry ticket holders were told that performances were being delayed for a few days because of "technical problems." The play never did open! The director, Charles De Sheim, resigned in protest and the Chicago black unit, shocked by the experience, turned to musicals and comedies.

The greatest criticism of the FTP productions was usually reserved for plays that ended with blacks and whites joining together. The idea of unity between the races struck many people as being communist-inspired and therefore against the good of the country. One play of this sort was Theodore Ward's *Big White Fog,* the story of a black man named Victor Mason who is frustrated by the lack of opportunity for blacks in America. This frustration leads him to join the Marcus Garvey movement, a real-life back-to-Africa movement founded in the teens of this century by Garvey, a West Indian. The Depression that follows the stock market crash of 1929 is hard on Mason and his family. They are about to be evicted from their apartment when a white friend of Mason's son organizes a group of white and black people to help the Masons stay in their home.

Although the censors couldn't find any obvious communist propaganda in the play, they were sure it was there somewhere. After only ten weeks, the production, a box-office success, was moved to a local high school. It closed shortly thereafter for lack of an audience.

In spite of their concern about communist propaganda, there were many more plays that the censors rated highly than plays that they suspected of subversion. This was in part because most of the FTP productions were comedies and light-hearted musicals. Whatever their focus, the black unit productions were generally of extremely high quality, and they dominated the headlines about the Federal Theatre Project. It is no wonder that the black units' productions were so good. They were products of years of pent-up energy and creativity. If the FTP had been allowed to continue, who knows what greater productions might have come forth? But the FTP ended in 1939, a mere four years after it had begun. It was ended by the action of Congress, and if some Congressmen had had their way it would have ended much sooner than that.

In order to understand what caused the collapse of the FTP, it is necessary to know how some Americans were thinking at the end of the 1930s. Ever since the establishment of the Union of Soviet Socialist Republics in the 1920s, a nation founded on the principles of communism, there had been concern that this new doctrine would infiltrate the United States. During the Depression years, the Communist Party did in fact gain in popularity with workers and intellectuals, causing great concern among those strongly opposed to its principles. In the late 1930s, America's anti-communist faction decided the time had come to strike out.

Next to labor union organizers, the most suspect group were the artists and intellectuals who lived, thought and behaved as they chose. Not much could be done about writers and artists who made their living independently. But artists and writers who were paid by the goverment were another matter. In 1938 Congress set up a Special House Committee on Un-American Activities, which immediately began an "investigation of un-American propaganda acitivities" in the United States. One of its principle targets was the Federal Theatre Project.

The FTP, the committee charged, had engaged in a variety of subversive activities. Its outspoken commentary on social and economic issues, they said, proved this clearly. FTP units were obviously communist-inspired. Worse still, the FTP made a policy of integrating its activities and even its social affairs.

It is true that there were Communists and people who were sympathetic to communism in the FTP, both in the white units and the black units. But the FTP was hardly, as HUAC member J. Parnell Thomas, a Republican from New Jersey, put it, "seemingly infested with radicals from top to bottom." Still, a majority of the committee agreed with Parnell and were willing to accept as truth almost all damaging testimony and to ignore the defenders of the FTP.

Those who believed in the Federal Theatre Project rallied to its defense, including the black organizations whose advice had been sought and heeded throughout the project's existence. Over 150 black organizations signed an affadavit attesting that blacks in the project had received equal treatment with whites. But this statement only confirmed the suspicions of the members of the committee who agreed with the statement of its chairman, Martin Dies of Texas: "racial equality forms a vital part of communistic teachings and practices." For the very reason that it had seemed so forward-looking, the FTP was doomed. The committee reported that the project was indeed subversive, and in 1939 Congress cut off all further funds. All across the country the theaters that had brought drama to the masses—presenting subjects they could relate to at prices they could afford—went dark.

In spite of the FTP's short life, its members could console themselves on two points. First, *all* the WPA projects ended in 1941, with the end of the Great Depression. Second, and more important, in its brief existence the FTP had made an important contribution. It had supported some 12,500 actors per year throughout the nation at better ($83 a month) and steadier pay than most had ever received before. From the small admission fees it charged, it had brought in close to $1 million a year at its peak, and had provided some 20-25 million people, the majority of whom had never before seen a play, with superb, innovative and original theater.

But that was small comfort for the blacks in the Federal Theatre Project. The FTP had meant something different to them than to their white counterparts. To the whites, employment in the FTP was basically a job to tide them over until the Depression ended and the commercial theater came alive again. For blacks, their jobs with the FTP were the only jobs they had ever been able to count on with any certainty. With these jobs gone, they faced an uncertain future. John Houseman was deeply depressed about the situation. As he wrote in his introduction to the O'Connor and Brown history, "I felt that little of lasting value had been accomplished. Negro playwrights were not appreciably encouraged or stimulated by our efforts and Negro actors (with a few notable exceptions) were held, for another twenty years, within the galling bonds of stereotyped roles. The black technicians we had developed were once again excluded from every professional theatrical union throughout the country. No black company came into existence and, for the next twenty years, no Negro audiences clamored for a continuation of the entertainment they had appeared to enjoy under the auspices of the WPA."

But black creativity and energy and desire to be in the theater did not really end. They simply went underground for a time, like a seed that is waiting for the spring sun to warm the earth and the spring rains to moisten it. The black theater would re-emerge.

7
"Cast Down Your Buckets Where You Are"

The Rise of the Pre-World War II Little Theater

For a lucky handful of performers, the exposure they had received in the FTP led to parts in non-FTP plays. Ethel Waters was one of these few. Ironically, she had never really worked in the theater until she got involved with the FTP; her background was on the nightclub stage. Yet, in 1939, the year the FTP ended, she was given the kind of prize role that other black actresses with long experience in the theater had never had the opportunity to play. Not that she didn't deserve the part; no one had worked harder at her profession than she had.

Ethel Waters

Ethel Waters was born in Chester, Pennsylvania, on October 10, 1896. As a child, she was big for her age, and she was expected to act grown-up long before she was ready to. She would remember years later how "I had to hide my need to be cuddled," and perhaps that is why she got married, briefly, at age 12.

There wasn't much room for dreams during Ethel's impoverished childhood. She knew from a very early age that about the most she could expect out of life was to become a lady's maid for a wealthy white family. Still, she did love to dance, sing and perform before an audience, and when she was alone she allowed herself the luxury of pretending that she was a great actress, recreating the roles she'd seen played by the black companies and vaudeville acts at Philadelphia's Standard Theatre.

One night, when she was 17, Ethel happened to perform at a birthday/Halloween party attended by the vaudeville team of Braxton and Nugent. The two men hired her as a combination singer and shake dancer for a salary of $10 a week, and her career in vaudeville was launched. For the next several years she traveled around the TOBA circuit, where she became quite popular for her singing of "St. Louis Blues." Popularity on the vaudeville circuits often led to club work in a big city like New York, but for some reason the only New York club that seemed interested in Ethel Waters was Edmond Johnson's Cellar at 137th Street and Fifth Avenue, which Waters used to call the "last stop on the way down in show business. After you worked there, there was no place to go except into domestic service." She stayed at the club for several years, a stay that was made easier by the fact that she was getting opportunities to make records. Finally, in the summer of 1925, she was asked to perform at the famed Plantation Club and her cellar days were over.

Waters had dreamed for years of appearing in one of the big Broadway musical revues that had become so popular ever since *Shuffle Along* had set the style. She finally decided to put up the money and create a musical revue of her own. A composer friend put together a series of sketches and the result was *Africana,* which opened at the 63rd Street Theatre. It did not do particularly well there, but it was successful enough on the road to keep Waters busy for more than a year. *Africana* was followed by roles in *Blackbirds*—another Broadway revue, which flopped—

Ethel Waters as she appeared in *Mamba's Daughters*.

and *Rhapsody in Blue*—which also did poorly on Broadway but, like *Africana,* was very successful on the road. A year or so later, Waters accepted a starring role in *As Thousands Cheer* and became the first black artist since Bert Williams to star in an all-white Broadway production. This role led to a role in another Broadway musical, *At Home Abroad,* which ran during 1935–1936.

All these roles were primarily singing roles. It was not until the Federal Theatre Project that Ethel Waters really got a chance to do anything serious or dramatic. Her FTP performance in George Bernard Shaw's *Androcles and the Lion* received excellent reviews and Guthrie McClintic may have seen her in this play. Or he may have simply decided, having heard her sing, that she was the right woman to play Hagar in *Mamba's Daughters,* the next play he was going to direct.

Written by Dubose and Dorothy Heyward, the white play-wrighting couple who had adapted *Porgy* for the stage, *Mamba's Daughters* is the story of a black mother, Hagar, and a grand-mother, Mamba, who are ready to sacrifice all for the sake of the third generation, Hagar's daughter. The young girl has fair skin and has inherited a beautiful singing voice from her mother. Both grandmother and mother realize that she is special and should be given a chance at a good life. Though they live in extreme poverty and are surrounded by violence, blackmail and sordidness, they manage to raise the girl like a fine lady.

Hagar is dull-witted in many ways. As gentle as a child unless deeply stirred, she is capable of great violence if she or her family are threatened. When her daughter is very small, Hagar kills a man. Years later, when a blackmailer threatens to reveal that she once committed such a crime, Hagar kills him and then herself in order to save her daughter and her mother from disgrace.

The role of Hagar is very difficult because it calls on the whole range of human emotions. Ethel Waters performed it superbly and received universal critical acclaim. Almost over-

Ethel Waters (seated center) in a scene from *Mamba's Daughters*.
(MUSEUM OF THE CITY OF NEW YORK)

night, she was established as a major dramatic actress. Although she was helped by an excellent supporting cast, including Alberta Hunter, J. Rosamond Johnson, Jose Ferrer, and Canada Lee, she deserved sole credit for playing a remarkable role in a remarkable way. Ironically, it would be ten more years before she would be offered another dramatic role, but when it finally came her way she handled it with the same mastery. Her performance as Berenice Sadie Brown, the black cook in Carson McCullers' *The Member of the Wedding,* was unforgettable. The play, which opened at the Empire Theatre in 1950, was made into a film three years later. By the time *The Member of the Wedding* was staged, Ethel Waters had made a name for herself in Hollywood films, and she turned down several film offers in order to appear in the play, which won the Drama Critics Circle award for Best American Play of the Year. She was the most successful black female entertainer of her time, and when she died on September 1, 1977, the entertainment industry lost a great star.

Ethel Waters was among the lucky few black performers who were offered roles on the Broadway stage in the years immediately following the end of the FTP. That does not mean that those less lucky quit the theater. On the contrary, having experienced what it was like to appear before the footlights, design sets, write plays, and do the many other things connected with the stage, black people certainly were not going to give up the theater. There was a great deal of black theater activity in the years before World War II.

One of the things blacks in the theater were doing as the 1940s began was creating new organizations. Among the first of these was the Negro Playwrights Company, founded in 1940. Its purpose was "to foster the spirit of unity between races, provide an outlet for the creative talents of Negro artists . . . and supply the community with . . . theatre reflecting the historical reality of the life of the Negro people." Owen Dodson,

Theodore Brown, Theodore Ward, Abram Hill, and Langston Hughes were among the active members.

Langston Hughes was involved in all kinds of theater ventures at this time. In 1938, he'd helped found the Harlem Suitcase Theater in an old building on West 125th Street. The troupe got its name because all the equipment could be squeezed into one valise. The aim of the group was "to present plays of Negro life applying especially to the Harlem community at prices no higher than neighborhood movies, with community actors, and with all profits returned to a sinking fund." Its first production had been of Hughes's play *Don't You Want to Be Free?*, staged without scenery or curtains and "in the round," the way Hughes had seen plays produced in Russia. Tickets for the play, which opened April 21, 1938, were 35¢, and performances were on weekends only, when working people could attend. The production was eventually moved to the basement of the 135th Street branch of the New York Public Library. Altogether, it played one hundred and thirty-five performances, the longest consecutive run ever in Harlem.

When the Suitcase Theater moved on to other productions, Langston Hughes went to California where he founded the New Negro Theater in Los Angeles. Its first production was *Don't You Want to Be Free?* He then helped found the Negro Playwrights Company, and by 1941 he was in Chicago starting yet another theater group called the Skyloft Players. Their first production was Hughes's new play *The Sun Do Move.* Unlike the New York and Los Angeles groups Hughes founded, the Skyloft Players were still active more than twenty-five years later.

Hughes's friend and biographer, Milton Meltzer, once wrote, "It began to look as though whenever he wanted a play produced, he started another group." But the real reason for Hughes's travels was probably that he was a wanderer by nature. He once told fellow author and playwright Richard Wright, "Six months in one place is long enough to make one's life complicated."

The American Negro Theatre

Not long after the Negro Playwrights Company came into being, another group was founded in New York. It was called the American Negro Theatre, and its two principal founders were a playwright named Abram Hill and an actor named Frederick O'Neal, both of whom had been associated with the Rose McClendon Players, an established and respected theater group named after the late actress. Together with about 18 other theatrical people the two men formed a group that would be a cooperative venture, emphasizing all phases of theatrical activity. Their main aim was to avoid the so-called "star system," under which one person overshadowed everyone else and was pampered because he or she was a star. The group chose the name of their organization with great care. The title American Negro Theatre, of course, is a clear statement of the make-up of the group. But the initials meant something too. A.N.T. spelled ant, and every group member pledged to work just as hard as those diligent little insects.

After getting permission to perform in the small theater in the basement of the 135th Street Library, the company started raising money to finance its productions. They held two variety shows, which not only served to raise funds but also helped to introduce the new company to the Harlem community. Their first production, Abram Hill's *On Striver's Row,* ran for five months in weekend performances. Their next offering, Theodore Brown's *Natural Man,* was also popular with Harlem audiences. But the group's biggest success came in 1944, with a play written by a white man and a production that attracted white audiences.

The play was *Anna Lucasta,* by Philip Yordan. After trying without success to interest white New York producers in what was originally the story of a Polish working family in a Pennsylvania industrial town, Yordan's agent had taken the play to Abram Hill and suggested that his ANT company adapt it. Hill

A scene from *Anna Lucasta*. (MUSEUM OF THE CITY OF NEW YORK)

agreed, and the play was reworked into the story of a black family. It opened in 1944 in the basement of the 135th Street Library with a gifted cast, including Hilda Simms as Anna, Frederick O'Neal as her brother Frank, and Alvin Childress and Canada Lee. It wasn't long before the production moved downtown. Important critics were attracted to its finely drawn characters and the humor and "social significance" the black company brought to it. *Anna Lucasta* continued on to Broadway, where it stayed for 956 performances.

Unfortunately, *Anna Lucasta*'s success wasn't good for the American Negro Theatre for two reasons. First, it meant that new people joining the group looked at the ANT as their ticket to Broadway. Instead of remaining an experimental theater, the ANT soon became a showcase with the tendency to stage plays by white playwrights. In fact, after 1945, all plays produced by the ANT were by "safe" (white) authors. The second way success harmed the ANT was by making it "think big" and waste valuable energy planning ways to expand into other areas.

In 1945, the ANT became the first black theatrical company to present a regular radio series. The show was aired on Sunday afternoons on station WNEW and the fact that the company was black was deliberately played down. It was only at the end of the program that the thirty-minute plays were identified as ANT productions.

Some months after the *Anna Lucasta* production, the ANT was asked to move from the Library Theatre. This meant that the company no longer had a rent-free place to perform. It went first to an Elks Lodge on West 126th Street and then to a loft on West 125th Street, unable to afford facilities as well suited to it as those of the 135th Street Library Theatre had been. None of its later productions approached the success of *Anna Lucasta*. By the 1950s the company was mainly doing variety shows because these were the types of shows that attracted the largest audiences and helped pay the rent.

Although the American Negro Theatre holds an important place in the history of black theater, it could have been much more important than it was. Had it lived up to its original purpose, it could have been a true people's theater. But the very star system its founders had sought to avoid destroyed its promise in the end.

The war years brought striking evidence that white producers had not completely forsaken the Negro, and that white audiences still enjoyed black musicals. In 1943 a musical show with an all-black cast opened on Broadway. Called *Carmen Jones,* it was an adaptation by Oscar Hammerstein II of the original opera *Carmen,* by Bizet, who in turn had based his script on a story by the French writer Prosper Merimée. The original Merimée story and Bizet opera are about a gypsy tobacco worker and the toreador she loves. *Carmen Jones* is about a black girl who works in a southern parachute factory and her relationships with two men: a military policeman from a nearby army camp and a prize fighter.

The show received high critical acclaim, for its music, performances and overall production. Many critics and audience members stated that after the first half-hour they forgot that the actors were Negroes. Since this was long before integration of whites and blacks in American society—indeed, long before any movement at all toward such integration—that was high praise indeed. Both *Anna Lucasta,* played by an all-Negro cast but based on a story that had no real color, and *Carmen Jones,* sung by an all-Negro cast but presented so effectively that many people forgot whom they were watching, were important steps forward for blacks in the American theater. But an even bigger advance had occurred a few years earlier with the production of a play called *Native Son,* whose underlying theme was the color bar and whose major actor was unmistakably black.

Native Son

Richard Wright, author of *Native Son,* had started out as a poet. He had become interested in the theater in 1936 while working as literary adviser and press agent for the black unit of the FTP in Chicago. Wright worked on many FTP productions and may even have written his two unpublished one-act plays during this time. As a literary adviser with the FTP he was asked by the Chicago YMCA to judge entries in a contest for plays on black life. One of the plays was Paul Green's *Hymn to the Rising Son,* and that is how Wright became familiar with Green's work.

Meanwhile, Wright had started writing novels and short stories. His first novel was rejected again and again, but his stories became so popular that Wright was anxious to get into other more challenging kinds of writing. In 1939, Theodore Ward, author of *Big White Fog,* adapted one of Wright's stories, "Bright and Morning Star," to the stage and the two set about finding someone to produce it. They approached Ethel Waters, one of the wealthiest black actresses at the time, but she was afraid the play's militant tone would offend white audiences. Wright never forgave her for turning him down.

Wright next turned his attention to a stage version of his short story "Fire and Cloud," which was to be staged at the Harlem Suitcase Theatre. Rehearsals actually began in August 1939, but the project fell through because of lack of funds.

Though he seemed unable to get a play produced, Wright was finally getting somewhere with another form of writing, the novel. When his highly acclaimed stories, *Uncle Tom's Children* , were published in 1939, he was already deeply involved in a novel called *Native Son.*

While *Native Son* was still being written, Wright's friend Theodore Ward expressed interest in doing a stage adaptation. Orson Welles and John Houseman were also interested in staging the story and Paul Green offered to do the adaptation with the collaboration of the author. Wright remembered Green's play from the YMCA contest and still considered it one of the most realistic plays ever written by a white man. He liked the idea that Green wanted his collaboration, and was sure that Welles and Houseman wouldn't have any trouble raising money to finance the production. Three months after the novel was published, Wright signed a contract to do the play with Green for production by Welles and Houseman.

Upon publication on March 1, 1940, *Native Son* almost immediately made Richard Wright a "great American novelist." It also made him the first black novelist to have his book chosen by the Book-of-the-Month Club. His powerful story, powerfully told, concerned what happened to a young southern black migrant to the northern ghetto.

Bigger Thomas is born in Mississippi but moves with his widowed mother and sister to the South Side of Chicago where they live in poverty and despair. Unlike in Mississippi, it is possible to go for weeks at a time without seeing a white person. Whites hate and fear the ghetto. The blacks in the ghetto hate and fear the outside white society.

When the Thomas family goes on relief, the Welfare Department finds Bigger a job as chauffeur to a wealthy white family. The young man is forced to enter the very society that oppresses him.

The Daltons (Mrs. Dalton is blind) consider themselves very liberal on racial matters. In fact, their daughter Mary fancies herself a radical. She embarrasses Bigger by trying to treat him as an equal. He is especially mortified when she and her communist boyfriend insist that he eat with them in a restaurant in the black ghetto where everyone knows him. Mary gets so drunk that evening that Bigger is forced to carry her upstairs to her room. Just as he is putting her onto the bed, he hears someone coming. Bigger is thrown into a panic. He knows he must not be found in a white girl's bedroom. In trying to keep Mary quiet, he accidentally suffocates her.

Accepting his act as murder, Bigger does everything he can

to cover up the crime, including burning the body in the furnace. But the crime has given him a real sense of power—the first he's ever really had—and he asks for a ransom from Mary's parents. He also commits a second murder, beating his girlfriend to death with a brick because he is afraid she will give him away.

Eventually, the remains of Mary's body are discovered in the furnace and there is a huge manhunt for Bigger. He is captured and sentenced to die. His lawyer, who works for the International Labor Defense, a communist organization, defends him brilliantly, charging that the whole society is guilty right along with Bigger; that by denying the young black man any chance of happiness or even dignity it is largely responsible for his violence and hate. Even more important than his lawyer's plan of defense are the changes that take place in Bigger during his trial. It is while waiting to lose his life that Bigger at last finds meaning in it. Consistently rejected and oppressed, he has been unable to form a positive relationship with another human being. During his time in prison, he takes the first step toward forming such human bonds, both with his lawyer and with Mary's boyfriend, who has forgiven him for the crime. In the end, although Bigger dies, in a sense he has been saved.

Native Son contained all sorts of controversial elements. It dealt with racism and communism and it dared to include a scene where a black ghetto youth murders a white, upper class girl in her bedroom. This was strong stuff, even in a novel. It would be even stronger as theater. Wright and Green worked hard to transform the 250-page book into a fast-moving and absorbing stage drama, and Welles and Houseman came up with all sorts of scenery and staging devices to maximize the intensity and symbolism of the play. A great deal depended on the actor who played the role of Bigger Thomas. Many better-known actors were passed over in favor of a Canadian-born former boxer, Canada Lee.

Lee, whose real name was Lionel Canegata, had considerable

Canada Lee in a scene from *Native Son*.

stage experience. He'd played Banquo in the version of *Macbeth* produced by the Harlem unit of the FTP. He'd also starred as Jean Cristophe in the unit's production of *Haiti*. Lee managed to express all the rage and suppressed violence in Bigger and at the same time to make him a very sympathetic character. He was supported by a fine cast of black and white actors, although the actress who was first selected to play Mary eventually left the show because she feared the unfavorable publicity playing the role might bring her.

Many people thought that *Native Son* was too strong for the stage. Some blacks feared that black servants would lose their jobs because their white employers would no longer trust them. Some whites disliked the idea of a white actress appearing in the arms of a black man. But despite these objections, the play opened on March 21, 1941, to tremendous critical acclaim. Canada Lee, who was highly praised for his performance, told *Negro Digest* in early 1945, "We're making history in the theater. The Negro has never been given the scope that I'm given in this play . . . and not as some butler-valet type, some ignorant person."

Native Son ran at the St. James Theatre until June 15, 1941. It then went on tour, playing the Apollo Theatre in Harlem to a very enthusiastic audience and going on to theaters in New Jersey, Philadelphia, Boston, Detroit, St. Louis and Milwaukee. It was a tense moment when the troupe crossed the Mason-Dixon Line to present the play in Baltimore, Maryland.

The Baltimore police would not let the company put up pictures of black and white actors side by side in the lobby. Nor could blacks in the audience sit where they pleased. Blacks were restricted to the second balcony. But there were no serious incidents. In fact, the white members of the audience got so involved in the drama and with Bigger that they actually cheered his lawyer's speech in his defense. The actor who played the part of the lawyer later told a reporter for *New Masses*, "You can't imagine what it means to say what you've always wanted to say and to say it precisely to the people it was meant for."

More than any other play, *Native Son* showed how far blacks had come in the theater. It was only 20 years since Miller and Lyles and Sissle had worried that Eubie Blake's bald head would be pelted with eggs because *Shuffle Along* contained a love song.

The United States entry into World War II had the same negative effect on American theater as had the country's involvement in World War I. People looking for entertainment were likely to go to one of the many patriotic motion pictures that Hollywood was cranking out. Broadway's lights weren't blacked out altogether, but little was being done there in terms of black theater. It was not until 1947 that another serious dramatic play by a black playwright would be presented on the Great White Way.

As had happened before when opportunities for blacks in the commercial theater were few and far between, black little theater seemed to become more ambitious and more creative during the early forties. The major black colleges—Howard, Spelman, Talledega, and Hampton Institute—were making good beginnings at little theater. At Tuskeegee, in Alabama, the tiny Bucket Theatre created by the extension division of the college flourished throughout the war years. The group got its name from a story once told by Booker T. Washington, founder of Tuskeegee Institute: Some sailors were adrift in a lifeboat off the coast of South America. They were suffering from thirst because they had drunk all their fresh water days before. When a steamer finally came along, the sailors pleaded with its crew to give them water. The answer came back: "Cast down your buckets where you are." The sailors were puzzled but did as they were told. To their surprise, the buckets came up full of fresh water, for they had drifted into the wide mouth of the Amazon River.

The point of the story was that, if you look, you will find

all that you need right around you. Applying that message to the stage, the people at Tuskeegee decided to create their own theater in an old broken-down store. The resulting Bucket Theatre served as a place where Tuskeegee students wrote plays that were performed for the local farmers, who often participated in the productions.

At war's end, Broadway became active again, and opportunities for blacks increased. In 1946, a musical, *St. Louis Woman,* written by two black writers named Countee Cullen and Arna Bontemps, was presented on Broadway. It gave a young singer named Pearl Bailey her first good Broadway role. But it was not until the next year that serious drama written by a black returned to the Broadway stage.

The play was Theodore Ward's *Our Lan',* and it did not start out on Broadway. It opened in the 1946–1947 season in the tiny, dingy auditorium of the Henry Street Settlement House in Greenwich Village. The Henry Street Settlement House had started back in the early 1890s as a community house, where the immigrants from Eastern Europe could learn English and useful trades and come together for social affairs. Over the years it had expanded its services to embrace other ethnic groups, and by 1911 under the directorship of Lillian Wald its activities included theater offerings. The Henry Street Playhouse presented some excellent plays, and *Our Lan'* was one of them.

The play was about the aftermath of the Civil War. The Union's General Sherman promises a group of freed slaves ownership of some islands off the coast of Georgia. After the former slaves have cultivated the land as their own, the government heartlessly reclaims it. The black farmers fight for their property, but they are beaten. Many are massacred; the rest are left homeless.

Presented in the stark setting of the Henry Street Playhouse, *Our Lan'* was a powerful statement against the injustices of life for black Americans. It was about a war that had taken place some 75 years earlier, but many people realized that the situation still applied. Black soldiers who had fought and died for their country in World War II had returned to the United States to face as much discrimination as ever. There was great unrest among blacks because of this. The play created enough of a stir to cause white Broadway producers to make the trip downtown to see it. Two of them, Eddie Dowling and Louis J. Singer, decided it would play on Broadway.

The Broadway version, which opened at the Royale Theatre in 1947, was a lavish production, complete with howling wind machines, thunder and lightning, floodlights and expensive scenery and costumes. Some black critics said the play had been stronger when presented simply. But the essence of the play was not lost, and though it had only a limited run, it brought serious black dramatic theater back to the center of American theatrical activity. *Our Lan'* earned Ward a Theatre Guild award before the play was ever produced, and he won a Guggenheim Fellowship after the play was staged. The production also helped to chip away at another taboo that inhibited black theater: it included tender love scenes between black characters.

But there was a great deal more progress to be made. In the spring of 1948, Miles M. Jefferson wrote an article for *Phylon,* a magazine published by Atlanta University, called "The Negro on Broadway, 1947–1948." In it, he pointed out that except for Ward's *Our Lan',* no shows written by blacks had made it to Broadway that season, and that even the Negro theater off Broadway wasn't much to be proud of. The American Negro Theatre, housed in the Elks' Club on West 126th Street in Harlem at the time, presented two plays, *Rain* and *The Washington Years.* The first was an adaptation of a play written by white playwrights and the second was also written by white playwrights. Other experimental theaters couldn't seem to find produceable plays by black playwrights either. The black actors and actresses in these plays were talented, but they were not getting enough opportunities. Even the two black musicals of the season, *Caribbean Carnival*—featuring dancer Pearl Primus and a company of West Indian and Negro dancers from the Katherine Dunham and Primus dance schools—and *Meet Miss Jones*—with a score by Fluornoy Miller—were, in Jefferson's opinion, hopelessly mediocre. Jefferson ended his article with a list of things that he felt were needed in the black theater if it was ever going to reach its full potential:

1. The luring of a director or two . . . from our Negro colleges to take over the supervision of the activity of the American Negro Theater in Manhattan. One hears of the excellent accomplishments of certain trained directors in the colleges. . . . Their wisdom and skill are sorely needed.

2. The production of just one *play (one won't greedily ask for more) based on a Negro theme with the virtue of a sense of humor. . . . More sunshine cast in dark places will work miracles!*

3. The renovation and re-opening, under intelligent and business-like auspices, of the Lafayette Theater in Harlem. The American Negro Theater in Manhattan needs a home.

4. Good shows written and directed by the skilled people with prestige for Lena Horne, Muriel Smith . . . Mildred Smith, Ruby Dee, Ruby Hill . . . and a few others.

5. A competent critic of the drama on one of the Harlem news sheets who would campaign for a drama renaissance in Manhattan for the Negro.

Although black theater in the 1940s seemed somewhat stagnant compared to the 1930s and the 1950s, the decade saw some important developments. Previously taboo subjects and behavior for blacks became possible to present. In addition certain off-stage developments should not be overlooked. It was in the 1940s that Actors Equity made some important steps toward desegregating American theaters, steps that would pay off in the 1950s. The ANT founder and actor Frederick O'Neal was a member of Actors Equity at the time. The labor union for actors was very liberal, he told this author. "When they first started in 1913 there was some kind of codification of the black members [some secret way to identify them as black]," he says, "but that was soon dropped. And AE was an early opponent of segregation."

By the 1940s most of the members of Actors Equity, white as well as black, had decided that their art was poorly served in segregated theaters. How could they present plays on black subjects, or plays with black characters, in theaters that would not allow blacks in the audience? At a meeting of Actors Equity, O'Neal recalls, "A resolution was introduced to the effect that we would not play the National [in Washington, D.C.] as long as that policy existed. There were about seven hundred members at that meeting, and the resolution was adopted unanimously . . . At that time the National was one of the most lucrative stops on the circuit."

At that time even white actors were lucky to have steady work a few weeks out of the year, so it took great character for all concerned to voluntarily cut themselves off from a guaranteed good run at the National. Not only did members adopt the resolution on moral grounds, they stuck to their commitment, even though the management of the National Theatre decided to close the theater rather than to integrate it. In 1952 when the National finally changed its policy, the AE pressed on. Frederick O'Neal remembers, "Then we adopted a resolution that we would not play any theater in the country that had a segregated policy. We like to think that we were the opening wedge in the drive against discrimination."

That wedge was being driven deeper as the 1950s wore on. Black resentment against discrimination and segregation was building, partly due to World War II and the Korean War that followed. Many, many blacks had fought and died in Europe and Asia, and those who made it home were unwilling to accept being treated as second-class citizens. Black playwright William Branch dramatized this attitude in his 1951 play *A Medal for Willie*. In it, a black mother named Mrs. Jackson is asked by a southern town to be part of a ceremony honoring her son, Willie, who has been killed in Korea. The dead soldier is to be awarded a medal for bravery posthumously. Mrs. Jackson takes part in the ceremony, but instead of reading the speech that has been prepared for her, she tells the assembled townspeople how hypocritical they are to give dignity in death to a young man whom they treated without dignity while he was alive.

As black resentment grew, black organizations directed their energies toward changing the American social system through its system of constitutional law. The first major breakthrough occurred when the United States Supreme Court ruled in 1954 that "separate but equal" education was unconstitutional. This meant that communities could no longer segregate their schools by insisting that black schools and white schools were equally good. School desegregation was followed by the Montgomery, Alabama, bus boycott. For almost a year, most of Montgomery's blacks stayed off the public buses to protest the arrest of a black woman, Rosa Parks, who had refused to give up her seat to a white man. The boycott was successful, forcing city leaders to change the seating rules on buses and to hire black bus drivers.

The Montgomery action also led to the emergence of one of the most important black leaders of this century, Martin Luther King, Jr. With other southern ministers, he founded the Southern Christian Leadership Conference to continue the drive for equality by ordinary southern black people that had been started with the bus boycott. The civil rights movement had begun in earnest.

Curiously, almost none of the rising black protest of the early 1950s was reflected on the stage. Theater, both black and white, was primarily engaged in revivals. In the aftermath of World War II, Americans seemed to yearn for the peaceful prewar days, a longing that expressed itself in revivals of plays from that earlier period, especially musicals. Many of the major black musicals of the previous thirty years were revived at that time:

Green Pastures in 1951, *Shuffle Along* in 1952, and *Porgy and Bess* in 1953. The Committee for the Negro in the Arts (CNA), which had been formed in 1947, came out against these revivals, especially that of *Green Pastures,* as examples of the continuing "refusal of Broadway producers to present a true and honest picture of Negro life." But the CNA didn't go so far as to ask black performers and audiences to boycott these productions. The committee knew that jobs were scarce, and that black actors and actresses were being forced to take whatever work they could get.

The reason for the lack of stage roles for blacks in the early and mid-1950s was a curious one. As white playwrights and producers became more sensitive to racial discrimination, they realized that stereotyped stage roles like servants and comical characters were often racist. So they stopped including such roles in their plays. Unfortunately, they did not replace these roles with other parts for blacks, and it seemed as if the Negro was in danger of being eliminated from the stage completely. A variety of black theatrical and civic organizations felt something had to be done about this unfortunate situation, and in the early 1950s groups like Actors Equity, Chorus Equity, the Dramatists Guild and the League of New York Theatres were spurred by their black members to get together and draw up a statement, which read in part:

The theatre and all other expressions of American entertainment are today among the most powerful and influential media of communication and education. In a critical world period, when the democratic credo is under fire, it becomes increasingly important that the expanding role of our Negro citizens in the community of this nation be adequately portrayed in the entertainment arts. The realities of the American scene today confirm the portrayal of the Negro as a more general part of the scheme of our society, for example, as postmen, policemen, clerks, secretaries, government workers, doctors, and teachers, without the necessity of emphasis on Race.

The statement went on to say:

While caricature and stereotype are always to be condemned, there is nothing inherently wrong in comedy and servant roles when they are part of a living presentation. However, when the Negro citizens are presented exclusively in such roles, an imbalance results, and their integration in American life is improperly set before the world. We must correct this situation, not by eliminating the Negro artist, but by enlarging his scope and participation in all types of roles and in all forms of American entertainment—just as in American life, the Negro citizen's role now extends from the kitchen to the United Nations.

The statement was endorsed by many black and theatrical organizations, but it didn't have much direct impact on blacks in the theater. Their choice of roles remained very small indeed.

The really creative things that were being done in black theater in the 1950s were occurring off Broadway. Once again, in a time when the commercial theater seemed barren of new ideas and opportunities, community theater thrived. This time, however, Harlem was not part of the creative upsurge. The area had become increasingly slum-ridden and many of its once-great theaters had closed. The Apollo was the only major theater still in operation, but it did not offer dramatic presentations. Instead, it featured live musical performances, mostly of the new rock and roll variety.

The Greenwich Mews Theatre in Greenwich Village was one of the centers of black theater activity during this period. Alice Childress, William Branch, and Loften Mitchell were just a few of the black playwrights who saw their plays produced there. The Village as a whole was alive with artistic energy in the 1950s, and, as always when the most important concern is art, there was very little racism.

Prejudice seemed to be declining elsewhere in the nation as well. Spurred by Actors Equity and other groups that refused to abide by the old rules of segregation, white theaters were beginning to open up. Bit by bit blacks were becoming freer to attend downtown commercial stage productions. Now all that remained was for a downtown theater to present a show that blacks wanted to see.

Lorraine Hansberry's *A Raisin in the Sun,* which opened in 1958, was the play that blacks had been waiting for. Probably the best-known work by a black playwright, it won the New York Drama Critics Circle Award for the 1958–1959 season, was later made into a movie with the original cast, and has since been revived on Broadway.

Hansberry's play is the story of a black ghetto family whose members want a better life. The hard-working father has died, leaving an insurance policy to be collected by his family. The daughter, who is in college, wants the money for medical school. The son, who is married and working, sees the policy as a means of funding a get-rich-quick scheme. The mother has always dreamed of owning a house in a nice neighborhood and feels she should now have it. The plot is about how the family resolves its conflicts about the money, how the money is lost, and how the family finally comes together and agrees to work for the house in the nice neighborhood that will benefit them all.

A Raisin in the Sun contains a good deal of social protest, but the play is written with such skill and humanity that white audiences applauded the very criticism that was directed against them. Black audiences applauded it, too. By 1958 they were able to go into the Broadway theaters and buy tickets wherever they wanted to sit. They were more likely to try out integration because the movement for civil rights was growing, and they were more likely to have the money for theater tickets because black income levels and educational and employment opportunities were beginning to increase.

There were nights when the Broadway audience for *A Raisin in the Sun* was nearly half black. This was seen by many as

A scene from *A Raisin in the Sun*.

proof that blacks were slowly but surely moving into the mainstream of American life. There seemed reason to hope that eventually there would be no need for *black* plays and *white* plays; that someday there would be just one theater, intended for the people of a united America.

8
"A Hunger for Truth"

The Theater of Protest, the 1960s

In 1960, two students at the black Agricultural Technical College of North Carolina decided to desegregate the lunch counters in the area. When they were refused service at Woolworth's, they stayed there all day and were waiting outside the store the next morning when the doors opened. Within a month, eleven states were involved in such "sit-in" actions. During the next eight years, southern blacks, with help from northern whites and blacks, would revolutionize the legal and social structure of the South. Singing "We Shall Overcome," civil rights protesters would desegregate public facilities, including restaurants, stores, and interstate transportation, and would stage voting-rights campaigns. But they would pay a terrible price for the rights they eventually won. They would be attacked by police dogs, knocked down by jets of water, beaten, and jailed by the thousands. Some would even be killed. But until the mid-1960s, the civil rights workers did not fight back. Instead, they did their best to practice nonviolence as preached to them by the ministers of the Southern Christian Leadership Conference. The black plays of the early 1960s reflected this attempt at restraint and compromise.

The burst of civil rights activity in the early 1960s was accompanied by a burst of black creative activity. Black artists felt the need to express in their work what was going on in the South. Spurred on by the success of *A Raisin in the Sun,* many believed that the time was right to present black plays that would have meaning to both black and white audiences. Ossie Davis was among those who held that belief. In the late summer of 1959, he had joined his wife, Ruby Dee, in the cast of *A Raisin in the Sun,* replacing Sidney Poitier. At the time he had said, "At this point in this country there is a heightened interest in who the Negro really is. There is a hunger for the truth. It is incumbent on the Negro writer to begin to do the spadework. The hunger comes from both sides. There is the hunger of the American public for the truth and an overwhelming desire on the part of the Negro to express the truth about himself." In fact, Davis was hoping to help reveal that truth in a play he was then writing, *Purlie Victorious.* He had chosen to express himself through a form that would not offend anyone: comedy.

Ossie Davis and Ruby Dee— and *Purlie Victorious*

Although each has succeeded on the stage independently, Ossie Davis's and Ruby Dee's names are constantly linked together. They have done much of their most important work in the theater as a team, and are unquestionably the most influential black couple in the theater today.

Ossie Davis was born December 18, 1920, in a small town near Waycross, Georgia. When he was accepted at Howard University in Washington, D.C., after completing high school, he traveled all the way from Georgia to the nation's capital on foot. At Howard, Davis came under the influence of Professor Alain Locke, one of the foremost spokesmen for black arts, who had coined the term "New Negro" in the 1920s. When Davis said he was interested in literature and especially in writing for the theater, Dr. Locke advised him to learn all he could about the stage before trying to write for it. Davis took that advice. Armed with a letter of introduction from Dr. Locke, he traveled to Harlem, joined the Rose McClendon Players, and spent the next three years working in all phases of production and performing a variety of roles. He then joined the American Negro Theatre and began establishing himself as an actor. But he never forgot that playwrighting was his goal.

After serving as a U.S. Army Surgical Technician in Liberia, Africa, during World War II, Davis was transferred to the Special Services. It was here that he got his first opportunity to write and produce shows for his fellow soldiers. Unfortunately, his Army experience didn't help him much at war's end. There was very little demand for black playwrights and producers in the mid-1940s and Ossie Davis had to go back to acting.

Davis made his Broadway debut playing the title role in *Jeb,* a postwar social protest play that questioned why black soldiers who'd risked their lives to preserve the freedom of others had to return home to face the same discrimination as before. The play was fresh and sincere, and Ossie Davis was memorable in the leading role, but the play was a failure on Broadway, as were most plays that dealt with the problems of returning black soldiers after the war. However, the role gave Davis a chance to reach a wider audience, if only briefly, and it brought him together with a young actress in the cast named Ruby Dee.

Born in Cleveland, Ohio, in 1924, Dee grew up and was educated in New York. She became interested in the theater during high school and that interest grew when she entered Hunter College. While studying languages at Hunter she joined the American Negro Theatre, where she attended classes and did various odd jobs while waiting for a chance to appear in an ANT production. Her first professional break came in 1942, when she played a bit part in the ANT version of *South Pacific* starring Canada Lee. Her next role was in *Jeb,* where she met her future husband.

Ruby Dee and Ossie Davis. (MUSEUM OF THE CITY OF NEW YORK)

During the years that followed *Jeb,* Dee and Davis worked both together and individually to make their mark in the theater. In 1946, Dee played the title role in the Broadway revival of *Anna Lucasta,* and when she later toured with the show was joined in the cast by her husband. With the money he earned from that tour, Ossie Davis decided to take a course in play-wrighting. Ruby Dee went on to a featured role in *The Smile of the World* and her husband gave up his writing plans to join her in that production in 1948. In the early 1950s, both went to Hollywood, where they appeared with Sidney Poitier in the film *No Way Out.*

Despite his busy acting career in the years that followed, Davis never lost sight of his dream to be a playwright, and beginning in 1956 he wrote, staged, and appeared in a play each year in the Annual Negro History Week show for the Retail Drug Employees Union. He also had a play, *Alice in Wonder,* produced in Harlem in 1952 in a triple bill with two other plays written by black author Julian Mayfield. Davis's play received enough praise to cause him to expand it into a full-length play called *The Big Deal,* which was produced in Harlem in 1953. Only a few close friends knew that he was working on a second play at the time. He hoped that it would be a major work and he planned to devote as much time to it as was necessary to ensure its success.

In the winter of 1959–1960, Ossie Davis decided that his play was ready to stage. His friend, the director Howard Da Silva, was so excited after reading it that he took it immediately to Philip Rose, who had produced *A Raisin in the Sun.* Rose was equally enthusiastic and in September 1961, *Purlie Victorious* opened at the Cort Theatre on Broadway.

The play is about a wandering black preacher named Reverend Purlie Victorious Judson who returns to the South to establish a church of his own. He ends up in a small rural community in southern Georgia, where things haven't changed much since slave days. Nearly everything in the area is either owned or controlled by Ol' Cap'n Cotchipee, a white cotton plantation owner who has allowed the only black church in town to be turned into a bar. Led by the Reverend Judson, the black community tries to get five hundred dollars to buy an old barn and convert it into the Big Bethel Church. As it turns out, Ol' Cap'n Cotchipee has provided exactly the needed amount in his will for a black woman named Cousin Bee, who has taken care of him for years. When Cousin Bee ruins things by dying before the Cap'n does, Reverend Judson decides to substitute an ex-maid named Lutiebelle Gussie Mae Jenkins for Cousin Bee. He doubts that the Cap'n will know the difference, since "white folks can't tell one of us from another." But Lutiebelle gives herself away and the plot is discovered.

Purlie Victorious Judson and the other blacks then try to get the money through the Cap'n's son, Charlie, who in his father's opinion has recently shown disgracefully liberal tendencies. Charlie not only steals the $500 from his father but also has the deeds to the church drawn up in Purlie's name instead of his father's. When the old Cap'n learns what has happened he literally "dies on his feet." Out of respect, he is buried standing up. Then the black community joyously goes about reestablishing its church.

Davis himself admits that the play contains many stereotypes, including a white massa type, an Uncle Tom, an Afro-American nationalist, and a "liberal" white southerner. The play contains other elements as well that "would be offensive in the hands of a white writer," as he puts it. At the outset, he couldn't be sure that they weren't offensive in the hands of a black writer, too. But as Ruby Dee explained, "Everything's a risk. I don't see that you get anywhere without taking risks."

Dee and Davis minimized the risk somewhat by taking the lead roles for themselves, since they knew exactly how they should be played. Davis took the title role. Dee played Lutiebelle Gussie Mae Jenkins. Their superb supporting cast included Beah Richards, Godfrey Cambridge and Alan Alda.

Purlie Victorious was a hit on Broadway. In 1963 it would be made into a movie called *Gone Are the Days,* and in 1970 it was revived on Broadway as a musical called *Purlie.*

While Ossie Davis and others were trying to express truths that needed to be told by way of the commercial theater, other blacks were trying to do the same in the noncommercial, regional theater. Many black civil rights activists believed that the arts could be used to educate people in political consciousness and that an educational program should go hand in hand with the freedom movement. They felt that it wasn't enough to get black people to register to vote; these new voters had to be taught why casting a ballot was so important. The best way to educate them was to present plays that showed what happened to black people when they had no control over the decisions that affected their lives, or to stage dramas that showed what happened to black people who could control these decisions. At the same time, a community theater would help bring people within a region together, thereby creating greater solidarity. It was for these and other reasons that the Free Southern Theater got its start.

The Free Southern Theater

In the winter of 1963, three blacks working in Jackson, Mississippi, decided to start a black theater there. Two of them, Doris Derby and John O'Neal, were field directors for the Student Nonviolent Coordinating Committee. The third, Gilbert Moses, was writing for the *Mississippi Free Press.* They all had been involved with theater in one way or another, and all believed that starting a black theater in Jackson would add an important dimension to the civil rights movement. According to Gilbert Moses, writing in *The Free Southern Theater by the Free Southern Theater,* "We also wanted to sponsor benefits in Jackson, and ask black stars and performers to appear. We wanted to open Jackson up, to bring people there who normally were outside of state control and police authority. We wanted freedom: for thought, and involvement, and the celebration of our own culture . . . We wanted [a theater whose] political aims reflected the political aims of the Movement at that time: integration . . . A large part of the excitement generated by the idea for the theater was centered around the fact that it would be integration operating in the deep South and integration operating in the mainly unintegrated American theater. So two . . . ideas were in conflict from the beginning: The development of a black style of theater . . . and an 'integrated theater,' based on preexisting structures."

The project was supported by established black stars like Harry Belafonte, Ossie Davis and Ruby Dee. Many white stars as well were willing to give money and advice. The FST's first production—*In White America* by Martin Duberman, which opened in the summer of 1964—played in a number of Mississippi towns. It was to have been presented twice in Meridian, Mississippi, but the first show was cancelled because of a memorial service for three civil rights workers, two white and one black—Andrew Goodman, Michael Schwerner, and James Chaney. The three young men had been slain while investigating the possibility of starting a voter registration drive in the area.

The killings of Chaney, Schwerner, and Goodman reminded the members of the FST that bringing theater (especially integrated theater) to those who "had no theater" might be a risky enterprise. Many white southerners strongly opposed the idea, and FST members frequently experienced harassment. Some were evicted from their apartments for participating in a "mixed group." Others were arrested and charged with "vagrancy" when they tried as a "mixed group" to buy beer in a public bar. Local newspapers refused to review FST productions; local schools and auditoriums refused to give them rehearsal space.

But the FST kept on, and continued to attract talent. Black

actress Denise Nicholas, who would later play the part of the guidance counselor on the TV series "Room 222," was part of the company for a time. White actress Trish Van Devere, now married to actor George C. Scott, also joined the FST for a while.

By 1965, the harassment had become so great that the FST was forced to move to New Orleans. Joined by black poet Tom Dent, it expanded its activities to include more workshops, and almost by accident it also expanded the form of its offerings.

The matter of form had been a subject of serious discussion within the FST from the start. Its very first play, *In White America,* caused great controversy within the group, because although the play was black in terms of subject matter, it was not black in form. No one agreed exactly on what black form was, but it was generally thought to include more music and more spontaneity than was found in traditional plays. The controversy about form subsided somewhat as the FST ceased to be integrated. By 1964–1965, a change had come about in the civil rights movement. There was less focus on integration, less interest in working with whites. Young blacks, especially, believed that this was their fight and they wanted to wage it alone. They were anxious to owe nothing to whites, even those whites who seemed to be nonracist. As the FST gradually became all black, it was increasingly free to pursue particularly black forms.

In 1968, dissatisfied with the material on hand, the FST decided to hold a workshop to develop original plays. What emerged instead was poetry. After some thought about what to do with this unexpected material, the group decided to stage a series of poetry readings at black arts festivals and other community events. At first, they read the poems in no particular order; but after a while it occurred to them to organize the verses by theme, such as black pain, the beauty of blackness, black power, and black assertiveness. Finally, they began to introduce a kind of call-response pattern into the readings. As one player read a poem, other troupe members would comment on a line, or echo a question asked in the verse, or say "Amen." The end result resembled the dialogue that goes on between minister and congregation in a southern black church, or the interaction between a lead singer and a chorus. The audiences enjoyed it immensely. What they were witnessing was more than just poetry readings. "If not theater," said Tom Dent in *The Free Southern Theater by the Free Southern Theater*, "[it was] certainly something that was sophisticatedly theatrical . . . a giant breath of fresh air. We could deal with the same themes any play might, with just as much depth. It was simply that poetry seemed to be a *way* of perceiving the themes that Black audiences understood."

Unfortunately, in 1971, just as the FST was perfecting its poetry presentations, the group disbanded. But their ideas, their commitment to a special black theatrical form, and their experiments with presenting poetry in a theatrical manner would live on. Thanks to community theater groups like the Theater of Afro-Arts and the "M" Ensemble in Miami; Sudan and Urban Theater in Houston; Black Image in Atlanta; Dashiki in New Orleans; and teenage poetry ensembles in Greenville, Mississippi, the work begun by the FST would not be forgotten.

The summer of 1964 was a particularly violent time in the civil rights movement. Workers conducting voter-registration drives in Mississippi met with brutal resistance, as shown by the deaths of Goodman, Schwerner, and Chaney. There were so many beatings and jailings and so much white violence that many blacks began to feel that the pain and injury were just not worth it. They were tired of practicing nonviolence and not at all sure anymore that they wanted to integrate with people who either would rather kill blacks than allow them equal rights or were so hypocritical that they couldn't take a firm stand one way or the other.

There was a new militancy in the North as well, where poor,

ghetto-bound blacks were suffering severe discrimination in employment and segregation in housing and education. The rage they felt over their lack of opportunity finally erupted in major riots in several northern and western cities, beginning with the riots in Watts, the Los Angeles ghetto, in the summer of 1965.

The trend toward greater militancy was accentuated in the summer of 1966 when the major student civil rights group changed leaders. The new leadership immediately issued a call for Black Power. They still wanted equal rights, but they wanted to exercise their rights separately. These sentiments were echoed by new and even more militant groups in the West and North. The Black Panthers in Oakland, California, spoke of "picking up the gun" to get satisfaction, and the Black Muslims in Chicago preached that all whites were "devils" and talked of a separate black society.

The new emphasis on separateness and on Black Power gave rise to a new pride in blackness. This was reflected in such phrases as "Black Nationalism" and "Black is Beautiful." The very insistence on the word *black* was new. Until the mid-1960s, the term *Negro,* later seen as a white man's expression, had been preferred. The phrase *Afro-American* also became popular, as did the dashiki, the Afro hairstyle, and other things African. A number of blacks even took African names.

Black drama in the mid-1960s reflected these significant changes in the way black people viewed themselves and the larger society. Black playwrights were beginning to change the tone of their plays just as black civil rights activists were beginning to change their minds about integrating with whites. James Baldwin's play *Blues for Mr. Charlie,* written in 1964, reflects a shift toward these new attitudes. Based on the killing of a black man named Emmett Till by white southerners, it tells the story of Richard, a minister's son who returns home after many years in the North and acts so "uppity" that a white man murders him. The killer freely admits the crime and is put on trial. Baldwin uses the trial scenes to bring up many racial problems and suggests that their solution depends on the willingness of white liberals to practice what they preach.

Another major black writer, LeRoi Jones, disagreed with Baldwin's conclusion. He felt that white liberals could not be depended on and that reliance on whites was undermining the black struggle. This belief that blacks must make their way alone and on their own terms put Jones in the forefront of the separatist movement. Fully three years before the call went out for Black Power, and two years before the riots in Watts brought the new militancy out into the open, he was creating what later came to be called "drama of accusation."

Imamu Amiri Baraka (LeRoi Jones)

No one did more to bring about a truly black theater than Imamu Amiri Baraka. Born LeRoi Jones in Newark, New Jersey, on October 7, 1934, he took the African name by which he is known today in the late 1960s.

Baraka grew up in Newark and, except for brief periods away, he has devoted his life to improving conditions for the black community there. After receiving a bachelors degree in English from Howard University in Washington, D.C., he went on to do graduate work at the New School for Social Research and at Columbia University in New York City. His works of poetry and fiction helped to win him a John Hay Whitney Fellowship in 1961; but he was to choose drama as the means of expressing his steadily developing philosophy of the black existence in America.

In Baraka's opinion, the black American's real problem was himself—not for *being* a victim (he could hardly be blamed for slavery, discrimination, and segregation), but for *remaining* one. Baraka felt that plays were the best means by which to express this idea, and he concentrated on writing dramas that, as he told a writer for *Negro History Bulletin,* would "show victims so that their brothers in the audience will be better able to understand that they are the brothers of victims, and that they themselves are victims if they are blood brothers."

Baraka wrote *The Dutchman* in 1963. The whole play takes place in a subway car that is occupied by two passengers: a black man and a white woman. The black man, Clay, is a middle-class Ivy League graduate dressed in a three-piece suit. The white woman, Lula, is attracted to him, not because he is middle class, but because he is black. In fact, she wishes that he was lower class, because she thinks of black men as sexual, brutal, and easily attracted to white women. When Clay doesn't act as she hopes, she accuses him of turning his back on his people by becoming middle class. Clay warns her that he is just as capable of murder as the lower-class black of her imagination, but he makes no attempt to harm her. When Lula continues to challenge him, trying to force him to be brutal, he threatens violence if she doesn't leave him alone. But in the end, it is Lula who stabs Clay.

In *The Dutchman*, Baraka is trying to show that what happened to Clay is what happens to blacks who take on middle-class ways of thinking and behaving and expect whites to accept them. What they in fact end up doing is to leave themselves open to white violence and hatred and to allow themselves to be destroyed.

Baraka continued to express his philosophy of victimization in *The Toilet* (1964), which was produced the same year as Baldwin's *Blues for Mr. Charlie.* In this play, a group of black high school students gather in the school's men's room to beat up a white boy named Karolis because he has written a "love letter" to one of them. After the beating, Foots, the student to whom the letter was addressed, returns to the men's room, cradles Karolis in his arms, and cries. Foots is the black group's leader. By going back to Karolis, he shows that he is, in fact, "in love" with the system and with the very people who want to destroy him. He is a victim, too.

Walker, the main character in Baraka's play *The Slave,* also produced in 1964, is still another sort of victim. Formerly married to a white woman with whom he has had two children, he is now a revolutionary, convinced that he and his fellow blacks can never be free unless they kill all whites. When he returns to the home of his white ex-wife and her new husband, there is a violent confrontation during which he kills not only the husband, but also his own half-white children. In Baraka's view, any man who is forced to kill his own children is a victim, too.

The above three plays brought Baraka a great deal of attention. Most of the reviews were favorable. *The Dutchman,* which opened at the Cherry Lane Theatre in New York, won an Obie Award for the best Off Broadway play of the season. Instead of being scandalized or offended by his plays, whites, who made up at least half of the audiences, mostly welcomed Baraka's work. It was a way for them to get rid of some of their guilt over what whites had done to blacks in American history.

In reality, Baraka was not much concerned with what whites thought of his plays. His aim was to make his work available to as many blacks as possible. In trying to do so, he took up the call that had been sounded by W. E. B. DuBois half a century earlier and that had echoed on down through the decades since: blacks must have their own theater, by, about, and for themselves, a theater that did not depend on white models but would develop forms of its own. In an attempt to put into practice what he preached, Baraka helped found the Black Arts Repertory Theatre and School in Harlem in 1965. As he told *Ebony* magazine, its philosophy was his own: theater must mirror the actual life of the streets. "Pictures of black reality and black theater should be able to be exchanged easily . . . from stage to street without great disparity. The only difference must be the clarity and directness of the art." It had to be collective "in that it speaks about a people, using the images and tone and energy of that people." It had to be functional: "There is no such thing as 'art for art's sake.' . . . The function of our art must be to restore our people to their traditional greatness." Spirit House, a community theater later established in Newark, was based on this philosophy.

Unfortunately, neither the Black Arts Repertory Theatre nor Spirit House was successful, perhaps because Baraka was too involved with various civic programs to give them his full support. But he continued forcefully to express his philosophy of the black theater in the plays he wrote throughout the 1960s. *Experimental Death Unit #1* (1964) was followed by *A Black Mass* in 1965, *Madheart* and *Great Goodness of Life* in 1966, and *Slave Ship* in 1969. Although none of these later works had quite the same impact as *The Dutchman* did, most were praised by critics—if not for their subject matter, at least for their form.

Baraka is still working for his Newark community and still talking about radical change; but his influence on black theater belongs to that time in the middle to late 1960s when he was the foremost exponent of revolutionary theater.

Much black theater in the 1960s was labeled "revolutionary," and rightly so. The so-called black theater of earlier days had in fact been what critic Clayton Riley called an "American theatre of Negro participation." This meant traditional plays for traditional audiences: plays written and staged in the conventional way that just happened to be about black subjects and that, occasionally, just happened to be written by black playwrights, which audiences of middle-class people who could afford high ticket prices—audiences that just happened to include middle-class blacks—attended. But now, a real black theater was evolving, spontaneously and in a variety of places. Down South, people associated with the Free Southern Theater were experimenting with poetry readings as theater; up North, such playwrights as Baraka were producing what later came to be called the "drama of accusation." Other playwrights, such as Ed Bullins, were writing what was known as "the drama of self-celebration"—plays that expressed in one way or another the various meanings of the "Black is Beautiful" slogan. Everywhere new theaters and new theater groups were starting up.

Bullins was playwright-in-residence at the New Lafayette Theater, founded in 1967 by director Robert Macbeth. The New Lafayette, which took its name from the old Lafayette Theatre in Harlem, eventually found a permanent home in a converted movie house on Seventh Avenue near 138th Street, not far from the site of its namesake.

Bullins's plays, such as *In the Wine Time* and *Goin' a Buffalo,* perfectly expressed the philosophy of the New Lafayette Theater, which was determined to create and to maintain a distinctly black theater. His dramas did not rely on complex plots for their effectiveness. Instead, they depended on strong characterizations and on the kind of humor that would appeal to black audiences but that would puzzle most whites. The stated aim of the New Lafayette was to present drama by blacks about blacks for blacks in a Harlem theater that had no dependency on and owed no allegiance to Broadway or to white audiences. The New Lafayette Theater did, however, seek funding from white foundations and cultural-support groups.

The National Black Theatre, founded a year after the New Lafayette by actress and director Barbara Ann Teer, shared some of its predecessor's aims. The NBT also emphasized some of the basic goals of the earlier American Negro Theatre, stressing group rather than individual effort. Sound technicians acted, actors built sets, and lighting people danced in the chorus! But the NBT was far more militant than both the old ANT and the New Lafayette. Its primary goal was not to entertain, but to reeducate the black community, to raise its consciousness and restore the cultural tradition that, according to the NBT, had been stripped from blacks in America. The plays were not called plays but rituals or revivals. Music and movement, featuring African and West Indian dances, were integral parts of the performances. The actors were not called actors but liberators;

and the sections of the performances were not acts but "spaces." Intermissions were the one concession to traditional theater practice—but they weren't times for the actors to go off and rest. Instead, the players mingled with the audience, talking and joking.

The NBT was the most revolutionary theater and theater group to arise in the late 1960s, and if none of its presentations made headlines or got much critical attention, the management and performers didn't care. Unlike the New Lafayette, the NBT did not seek outside funding, for that would have meant compromising its philosophy, since all the major funding sources were white. It was a "low budget, no budget" group that staked its future on the Harlem community and the desire of that community to be reeducated through what it saw on the stage.

A third major black theater group to start in New York in the late 1960s was the Negro Ensemble Company. Unlike the New Lafayette and National Black theaters, it was not situated in Harlem but on Manhattan's Lower East Side. It also differed from the other two in its less restrictive philosophy. The individual artists were allowed greater freedom: the plays were to be primarily about black life, but good drama from other sources and about other people would not be excluded; the audience did not have to be all black. The NEC sought outside funding, and got it. The Ford Foundation made a grant to cover the company's first three years of operation, while the ensemble was still in the planning stage.

There was other activity in the drama field as the 1960s reached an end. Ed Bullins started a magazine called *Black Theatre* in 1968. A year before that, Amiri Baraka and Larry Neal, a black poet and critic, had published the first anthology of the movement, *Black Fire*. In 1969, Bullins edited an anthology called *New Plays from the Black Theatre*. Such books and magazines might not seem all that noteworthy except that just a decade or so earlier there were so few black plays that black theater

ble agenda" to give the award to a black playwright. They went on to say that, if this was indeed the case, Ed Bullins's *Goin' a Buffalo* or Lonnie Elder III's *Ceremonies in Dark Old Men* was more deserving of the prize for best American play of the year. There are almost always charges of "politicking" surrounding award-giving, but keen observers of the black theater scene suggested that this kind of controversy over a black playwright's award showed that black theater and the black theater movement were still on shaky ground.

True, there were more black productions on Broadway in the 1970s than at any time since the Harlem Renaissance: *Purlie, Raisin, Bubbling Brown Sugar, The Wiz, Don't Bother Me I Can't Cope, Your Arms Too Short to Box with God, Timbuktu!, Ain't Misbehavin'*. But with a few notable exceptions, they were all either revivals or musicals. The big musicals were splashy and full of energy, but they were no closer to picturing black life than the Sissle and Blake and Williams and Walker musicals of half a century earlier. *Ain't Misbehavin'*, which won a Tony for the best musical play of the year, didn't even have a plot line.

This is not to say that there is no place for musicals, with or without plot lines, in the theater. It does suggest, however, that a theater is more than an oversized nightclub and that it offers possibilities that are only partially exploited by such musicals. It should be noted here that white theater fare on Broadway in the 1970s was as limited as the black productions, featuring such revivals as *The King and I* and *Oklahoma!*, and such big musicals as *Annie* and *Evita*. More often than not, daring, creative theater, both black and white, in the 1970s and today is found primarily in Off Broadway and Off Off Broadway theaters.

The main reason for this is economics. Salaries, production costs, strong stage unions, and high rents have forced the big commercial theaters to become even more commercial. Financial backers of shows, called "angels," invest their money not for the sake of art, but with the hope of a substantial return on their investment. Ticket prices have risen out of the range of

A scene from *The Wiz.*   (MUSEUM OF THE CITY OF NEW YORK)

many people, while those who can afford to go to a play often do so only occasionally. When they do decide to pay their $14 to $35 a seat they too want a "return on their investment." The larger and more lavish the production, the more likely the audience is to leave the theater thinking that, whatever the cost of the ticket, it was money well spent.

Because of all these factors, Broadway is no longer "where it's happening" in the theater. This will continue to be true as long as money is all-important there, especially in terms of black theater. For all the black visibility on that famous street, it remains very much the Great *White* Way. Nearly every Broadway production has white financial backers behind the scenes; but there are no black "angels." This means that black playwrights and black producers who want to take their shows to Broadway are not entirely free to do what they want. What few black plays there are on Broadway that can claim to have gotten there without white influence did so via Off Broadway and Off Off Broadway. White financial support does not automatically bring white influence, and white influence does not automatically mean a lack of honesty or realism, but for a true black theater to exist there must be black financial backing as well as white. Black theater should be able to continue even if white funding were somehow to be cut off entirely.

What are the other "shoulds" of a true black theater? W. E. B. DuBois listed them back in the early part of this century as we saw in Chapter 5. In DuBois's day, few if any of his fundamental principles for a Negro theater movement had been fulfilled. What is the situation now, over a half a century later?

DuBois wrote that black theater must be *"About us."* When he stated this, there were no plays being produced that presented real black life. Judging from what was being shown on the stage, black Americans spent their lives singing and dancing and "shuffling along." They were never sad, except in a comical, clownish way; they were never angry; they did not love like white people did. In contrast, the American theater now can function as a stage for real black life, and has served to mirror black hope, despair, anger, love, antiwhite feeling, and self-hatred. In plays ranging from Ossie Davis's *Purlie Victorious* to LeRoi Jones's *The Dutchman,* the spectrum of black behavior and black feeling has been presented, and a balance between the two extremes has been achieved. Black plays today need not be deliberately comical or self-consciously revolutionary; they can be unself-consciously real.

DuBois wrote that the second principle for an American black theater was that it be *"By us."* He did his best to encourage the development of good black playwrights, of which there were very few, by conducting contests and founding the Krigwa Players to present plays written by blacks. If he were alive today, DuBois would be amazed at the number of talented black playwrights at work. Probably the black playwright who would amaze him the most is a young woman named Ntozake Shange.

Ntozake Shange

Shange was born Paulette Williams on October 18, 1948, in Trenton, New Jersey. Her father and mother were professional people, and Paulette had an extremely sheltered and comfortable early childhood, first in upstate New York and later in St. Louis. When she was chosen in her early teens to be bused 15 miles across town to integrate a previously all-white school, her secure world was shattered. Hissed at and jeered, she was made to feel like an outcast by her new white fellow students. She later explained, "You can't raise somebody like they're regular and then have everybody acting like they're not and expect no problems."

At Barnard College in New York City, Shange majored in Afro-American music and poetry and married a law student. After the marriage broke up, she tried to commit suicide. Failing, she channeled her anger into the student protest, civil rights

Ntozake Shange. (MUSEUM OF THE CITY OF NEW YORK)

and black liberation movements, but she resented the way the men in those movements treated women. On graduating from Barnard she went to Los Angeles, where she earned a Masters Degree in American Studies at the University of Southern California and changed her name. Ntozake means "she who comes with her own things," and Shange means "one who walks like a lion."

While teaching Women's Studies at Sonoma State College, Shange began writing poetry in earnest, which she would read at local bars. Eventually, she and choreographer friend Paula Moses began to work together, producing what Shange called a "choreopoem." The two moved to New York in 1975 and began performing in lofts and bars and lower East Side poets' hangouts. Black producer Woodie King, Jr., saw their work and determined to stage it. The show, directed by black director Oz Scott, opened at the Henry Street Settlement's New Federal Theatre on East 3rd Street in November 1975. It was called *For Colored Girls Who Have Considered Suicide/When the Rainbow Is Enuf.*

The show is composed of seven young black women, bareheaded and barefoot, each wearing a simple cotton dress of a different rainbow color. Together they present the real and the stereotypical images of the black woman—her wants and needs, her vulnerability and her humor—through music and dance and poetry. Shange herself was among them. In many ways, the "choreopoem" was her story, because by now she had not only "considered suicide" but had tried it four different ways before deciding to go with the rainbow instead. "The rainbow is: just the possibility to start all over again with the power and the beauty of ourselves. . . . Rainbows come after storms; they don't come before the storm."

For Colored Girls was generally praised by the critics and it was very popular with black audiences. It won several awards, including the Outer Critics Circle award, and attracted the attention of Joseph Papp, who produced the show in June at his

A scene from *For Colored Girls.*

New York Shakespeare Festival's Anspacher Theatre. After three months, Papp decided to gamble and take the show to Broadway. It opened at the Booth Theater in September and played for two years, the first play by a black woman to be staged on Broadway since Lorraine Hansberry's *A Raisin in the Sun.*

Shange was in the cast when it first reached Broadway, but she stayed for only one month. She then left to devote herself to writing her second major work, *A Photograph: A Study of Cruelty,* which Papp produced at the Off Broadway Public Theatre in the 1977–78 season. Called by Shange a "poemplay," it was about a black woman dancer who lives with a gifted but unsuccessful black photographer who takes out his bitterness and frustration on her. The critics compared it unfavorably to *For Colored Girls.* According to one reviewer, the new presentation required a formal dramatic structure and Shange had not provided it. "[She] is something besides a poet, but she is not— at least not at this stage—a dramatist. More than anything else she is a troubadour."

Another of Shange's poemplays, *Spell #7: A Geechee Quick Magic Trance Manual,* was produced in early 1979. Once again, it was compared unfavorably to *For Colored Girls,* but it got better reviews than *A Photograph.* In fact it was sufficiently well received to make some people think that Papp might take it to Broadway. But as Papp explained, "A lot of white audiences are receptive to black musicals, but not serious black plays. Everyone thought it was risky when we moved Ntozake's 'Colored Girls' to Broadway—and that was when the tenor of the times was much less conservative."

Shange continued to pursue her craft, and to learn more about the theater. In the summer of 1979, she had her first directing job with *The Mighty Gents,* which toured New York City on the Shakespeare Festival Mobile Theater. Then she turned her attention to an adaptation of white playwright Bertolt Brecht's *Mother Courage,* shifting its setting from seventeenth-century Europe to the American southwest. The play, which tells the true story of how four black infantry regiments opened the area to settlers after the Civil War, starred actress Gloria Foster in the title role.

By staging a classic like Brecht's, Shange gained experience with the kind of formal dramatic structure that may influence her future work. Whatever way she chooses to use her ability, she remains one of the most exciting personalities in the black theater today and is expected to do more daring, creative work in the future. But if, as Joseph Papp puts it, white audiences remain unwilling to support anything but black musicals on Broadway, she will not have a chance to reach such a wide audience again.

"For us" was DuBois's third principle for a black theater. By this he meant that black theater should be primarily for black audiences, both financially and artistically. In DuBois's day, as we have seen, even the big black musicals were attended primarily by whites, but things are different today. The emergence of a black middle class has created a theater audience that can afford to see at least an occasional play and that likes theater and is comfortable with it. But so far this black middle class has not shown a willingness to be the sole support of a distinctly black theater and is not theater-oriented enough to provide the only audience for black theaters. Hopefully, this situation will change. As Vinnette Carroll, director of such Broadway hits as *Don't Bother Me I Can't Cope* and *Your Arms Too Short to Box with God,* puts it, "We certainly have a group of black people now with the money to invest in the theater, so that they can see positive images of themselves and have positive images of their children. I would like to see black people have the faith in themselves to trust us with their money."

Until that time comes, black theater institutions will have to rely on white support. Those that have refused this support have not lasted. Survivors, like the Negro Ensemble Company, have not only accepted white aid, they have actively sought it.

The Negro Ensemble Company

The NEC grew out of the Group Theatre Workshop, which was started in 1962. The workshop began on a very small scale, but as actor Robert Hooks, one of its founders, told producer Woodie King in King's film documentary on black theater, there was so much interest among young blacks in the theater movement and such a need for a theater company, that it soon attracted a great deal of talent. "The young kids started coming from Harlem and Bedford Stuyvesant and Jamaica [Queens] and before we knew it we had a theater. One of the first financial contributions we received was from Langston Hughes. I wanted to show the community, the parents, what the kids were doing, that they weren't just coming to jive around with this actor guy who was doing this Dutchman play. [At the time, Hooks was appearing in LeRoi Jones's *The Dutchman.*] So we put on a production of skits and improvisations and we did a one-act play called *Happy Ending.* It got such good reviews in the papers the next day, and we didn't even know the critics were coming; it was just a thing for the parents and the community. But I said, well, if the play like that got that kind of reviews with these young amateur actors, then I could put the companion piece with it and really have something. I'm talking about *Happy Ending* and *Day of Absence,* Douglas Turner Ward's double bill that is now a classic."

The two Ward plays opened at the St. Mark's Playhouse in the fall of 1966 and ran for well over a year. According to Ward, so many black actors appeared in the production over the course of its run that it became almost like a fraternity for black stage talent of the time. "The need for the Negro Ensemble Company arose out of the fact that it was quite clear, just as it was in real life at that time—the whole struggle for autonomy, for independent black institutions—that there was an absolute crying need for a theater. And with the Group Theatre Workshop we had all the ingredients for a model black theater institution." Hooks, Ward, and Gerald Krone, who had managed the Ward productions, then went about establishing that model black theater institution.

The stated purpose of the Negro Ensemble Company was to establish a theater of "permanence, continuity, and consistency providing the necessary home base for the Negro artist to launch a campaign to win his ignored brothers and sisters as constant witnesses to his endeavors." In less fancy language, this meant that the NEC wanted to start a permanent black theater that would be of, by and for black people. The other black theater groups that were created around that time—Amiri Baraka's Black Arts Repertory Theater, the National Black Theatre, the New Lafayette Theater—shared this goal. But at the same time they felt that the theater was basically a political tool to be used to further black nationalist philosophy, while the NEC was much less rigid and separatist. As Larry Neal put it, the NEC's philosophy was more along the lines of the civil rights movement.

While the black nationalist theaters regretfully learned that their philosophy was too limited to ensure long-term existence, today, more than ten years later, the NEC can proudly state that it has achieved and continues to achieve its original purpose, or at least the major part of it. Though some outsiders would say that the NEC's output has not been especially consistent, the members of NEC would disagree. From the start, the company had intended to present a variety of work, from plays about black life to classics of world drama.

One reason the NEC is still in existence is the wide range of material it presents. Another is the funding that it has actively sought from sources such as the Ford Foundation and the Rockefeller Foundation—sources that some theater companies considered too "establishment" and conservative. Still another may be its location, for whites are more likely to attend performances in lower or midtown Manhattan than in Harlem or in Newark's black ghetto. This does not mean that the group is not still struggling along from one foundation grant to the next. As Douglas Turner Ward, the tireless director of the NEC, puts it, "I'm essentially a creator, but I have been forced to be a fund-raiser, a beggar."

In its first year, the NEC's offerings were boldly experimental. They included a play by a European playwright about Portuguese exploitation of blacks in Angola and an adaptation of an Austrian play to a Louisiana setting and involving black migrant workers. Great emphasis was placed on developing a permanent company of artists; and tuition-free workshops in voice, dance, and the technical aspects of the theater were soon established. In 1969, when the NEC was barely a year old, the company was awarded a Tony for developing new talent and audiences.

In terms of audience attendance, the NEC also got off to a good start. At first, the audiences were about eighty percent white. Whites were more accustomed to going to the theater; the NEC got a lot of publicity because of its Ford Foundation grant, and the stated purpose of the NEC appealed to liberal whites, giving them a chance to practice what they preached by supporting a new black theater company. After the novelty wore off, white attendance dropped, but the slack was taken up by blacks who were attracted by the NEC's promise and by the publicity the group received.

Not all the publicity was good. White critics, though generally supportive, were not sure how to view some of the plays that had distinctly black themes. They were sensitive to black charges that white critics were incapable of reviewing black creative efforts objectively, and in response they were either unduly harsh or afraid to commit themselves. At the same time, black critics tended to criticize the NEC because it wasn't revolutionary enough, because it accepted white foundation support, and because it kept the word *Negro* in its name when *black* was now the favored term.

The NEC's hopes and ambitions were further complicated by funding problems as white support began to diminish. The first Ford Foundation grant ran out after two and a half years, and by 1972, the NEC had been forced to cut back on its ambitious training programs, shorten its performing season, and disband its resident company. The 1972 season, which began late, consisted of exactly one play. Fortunately, that play was Joseph Walker's *The River Niger.* Ward directed and played the major role in it. Critics praised the play so highly that Ward decided to take it to Broadway. There it won a Tony award for best play of the year, and this in turn gave the NEC some relief from financial worries.

But there was still not enough money to revive the training programs of the early years, or the multi-play seasons. Many productions were done in workshop form only, and though they provided opportunities for young black talents to gain exposure and experience they were not the kind of productions Ward and the others wanted to present. It was still not possible to have a resident company, or even a small core of paid members. More and more often, Ward both directed and acted in the plays, to save money. The need for money also caused the NEC to come close to compromising its purpose as an alternative theater by looking too quickly to Broadway.

In February 1974 the first play of the 1973–74 season opened late, as usual. *The Last Breeze of Summer,* in which Ward both acted and directed, received excellent reviews and attracted large audiences, causing the NEC to move it to Broadway. Unfortunately, the move proved to be premature and the play soon closed, leaving the NEC to face its usual large operating deficit and new charges that it had tried to "sell out."

The NEC cannot be blamed for making a try at the big money brought in by a Broadway hit. However, if it is to retain its uniqueness, it must continue experimenting with new forms. In fact, despite a lack of money and personnel, the NEC seems to be becoming bolder and more certain in its experimentation. In the 1978–79 season, it managed to produce a total of four plays, including two that were artistically superb: Gus Edwards's *The Offering* and Lennox Brown's *The Twilight Dinner*. Both productions were excellent examples of a separate, distinct, and completely unself-conscious black theater, a kind of theater that does not depend on political fads, like the black nationalist theater did, or on artistic fads, like the abundance of black musicals that were presented on Broadway in the late 1970s and early 1980s. As proof that the NEC can hold its own in the face of Broadway musicals, one need only look at a play like *Home* by Samm-Art Williams.

Williams's play is an example of what a company like the NEC can do best. It is modest in cast and staging. There are only three actors, and because it revolves around a middle-aged man sitting in a slat-back rocking chair on the front porch of his farmhouse, the production requires little in the way of props or scenery, drawing its strength instead from fine acting and important truths powerfully presented by a talented playwright.

Home tells the story of a southern farmboy, Cephus Williams, who wanted nothing more than to till the soil and marry his sweetheart, Pattie Mae Wells. But as he grew into adulthood, events changed his life. His uncle and grandfather died, Pattie Mae decided to look for a better life up North, and Cephus was drafted. When he refused to serve in Vietnam on religious principles, he was jailed. On his release from prison he decided to follow Pattie Mae up North, where he didn't find the "good life" any more than she did. By the time he boarded a bus back to Cross Roads, North Carolina, he was exhausted and looked like a bum. But he forced himself to stand tall and tried to look prosperous for the folks back home. "The North is supposed to be good for you," he explains to the audience. "I don't want to damage the myth."

A scene from *Home*. (MARTHA SWOPE)

Back home, sitting in his rocking chair, Cephus Williams tells the story of his life, and though it is a sad story in many ways, the play itself is a comedy, because of Cephus's outlook on life. It is full of stories of his boyhood: about his friends Joe Boy, Hard Headed Herbert, and One-Arm Ike who lost his arm while trying to steal Sydney Joe Murphy's hogs; about young love and his desperate attempts to romance Pattie Mae in a hay loft. Moving on to his time up North, he draws a comical picture of a southern farmboy in the cold and sin-filled big city and shows, in an indirect but convincing manner, that he is a man who needs his roots and is happiest and most contented at home.

Home is a distinctly black play about the black experience. It is also distinctly American. But it also has a universal appeal, because in its quiet, humorous way it conveys essential truths about life and love and purpose. It is the kind of black theater that can proudly take its place among world theater of all origins.

When first presented at the Negro Ensemble Company playhouse, *Home* was a modest production by financial necessity. There were just three actors. Charles Brown played Cephus Williams, with two women, L. Scott Caldwell and Michele Shay, playing several characters each. Caldwell took the part of Pattie Mae Wells, as well as assorted country girls and city women. Shay played everything from a wide-eyed farmboy to a prostitute to a social worker to a soldier on the front line in Vietnam.

When it was decided to move the production uptown to Broadway's Cort Theater, a few major changes were made. The NEC could have added more actors had it chosen to do so, but it did not. The farmhouse porch set was enlarged to fill the larger stage, but no additional sets were built. Yet when the bright lights of Broadway were turned on *Home,* the production did not look insignificant and out of place. As Mel Gussow wrote in the New York *Times,* "Downtown at the Negro Ensemble, 'Home' was marked by its warmth and intimacy. On Broadway, impressively restaged . . . the play retains both of those qualities. Unlike some plays, it does not dwindle in the Broadway spotlight. The language and the emotions are grand enough to fill a bigger theater.''

A score of other critics were equally effusive in their praise, and in the late spring of 1980 New York newspaper readers were treated to an uncommon sight: full-page ads for an NEC play on Broadway. Again, some were quick to cry "sell-out," but Douglas Turner Ward and the others of the NEC insisted that the profits from *Home* on Broadway would be used to finance more of the experimental, non-commercial plays on which the troupe's major reputation is based.

Profits from *Home* helped the NEC move to new, expanded quarters on West 55th Street and helped to finance its next major production. Charles Fuller's *Zooman and the Sign,* which opened in September 1981, was in the best NEC tradition. Wrote New York *Times* critic Walter Kerr, "Flaws and all, I found 'Zooman' more satisfying than most of the other serious work I've attended this year.''

It is true that the Negro Ensemble Company has not completely lived up to its original purpose. Its most serious failure remains its inability to develop a much needed permanent resident acting and directing company for young blacks. It has, however, managed not to sell out to commercial interests and to make a real mark on the theater world. Moreover, despite its shortcomings, it is the one and only black theater company with a national reputation.

W. E. B. DuBois concluded his listing of fundamental principles for a black theater with a fourth requirement: *"Near us."* This condition has not yet been met. That is not to say that successful black community theaters do not exist. One venerable example is Karamu House in Cleveland, which at more than sixty years of age is still as vital as ever. Its performing-arts season is one of the most extensive in the country among community arts centers, and it can point to a number of people who started there as volunteers and went on to make names for themselves in television, films, and theater. Beginning with Langston Hughes, successful graduates have included Ivan Dixon, Greg Morris, Saundra Sharp, Ron O'Neal, and Robert Guillaume. The people at Karamu House believe that their program can continue for another sixty-plus years, as long as they continue to be pioneers in the tradition of Karamu House's founders.

Unfortunately, unlike Cleveland, there are many cities with large black populations capable of supporting community centers and community theaters of their own who have nothing like Karamu House. Many talented blacks are working today to change that situation, and more and more people who are concerned with black theater are becoming optimistic about the chances of their success.

One is Woodie King, Jr., a black producer who helped to found the New Federal Theater of the Henry Street Settlement House. Once populated primarily by Jewish immigrants, the Henry Street area was predominantly black and Hispanic by the time King joined the settlement house staff in 1970. King set about bringing the theater and its new community together, and over the next decade he introduced the work of such important playwrights as Ed Bullins, Ron Milner, Ntozake Shange and Charlie Russell to New York audiences. Several plays first presented at Henry Street have gone uptown, due in large measure to the professional relationship King has enjoyed with Joseph Papp, founder of the New York Shakespeare Festival and the Public Theater, who became artistic director of the Vivian Beaumont Theater at Lincoln Center. Ed Bullins's *The Taking of Miss Janie* and Ron Milner's *What the Wine-Sellers Buy* both went to Lincoln Center after opening at Henry Street and, as we have seen, Ntozake Shange's *For Colored Girls* made it all the way to Broadway.

King is keenly aware of the great progress black theater has made in the last twenty years. In 1976 he began filming a television documentary on the modern black theater movement; it was first aired on PBS in 1979. What he found in the course of making that film helped fuel his optimism about the vitality of regional black theater in America.

The first thing King discovered was that he couldn't just stay in New York to film his documentary. It was necessary to go to San Francisco, Chicago, Baltimore, Washington, D.C., and even to Bermuda to find and interview the people who seemed to be doing exciting, creative things in the black theater movement. He also found that, while most of these people were hoping to eventually get to New York, they were, in the meantime, committed to establishing viable black theaters at home. As Shauneille Perry, director and actress, explained in King's documentary film,

It seems to me that most of the black works currently enjoying what is called commercial success—Broadway—began, with the exception of The Wiz, *on the workshop level. Vinnette's [Carroll's] plays after all come out of her own theater.* Bubbling Brown Sugar *started on the workshop level. There are many others. Despite how people feel about it, ultimately everybody's aiming for Broadway, but the positive thing about the success of all these plays is that it shows black directors, actors, and so on that instead of waiting for the "big break," to be plucked out of wherever you are by whoever does the plucking, one must create his own avenue. You can't dwell forever in the negativeness of "Why wasn't it me? Why wasn't I picked? When is it gonna happen for me?" You have to do it. And that may mean in somebody's attic or loft or livingroom. You have no idea where it might go. I firmly believe that. It's been proven over and over again. In fact, for us [blacks] it may be the only way.*

King believes that this is a healthy attitude, and he found it over and over again in the cities to which he traveled to make his documentary. He says:

171

[Regional black theater] is a national movement. All the major institutions recognize it as viable and on-going. But it had to move out of New York to achieve that recognition. In this respect, it is like black dance. When black dance got away from New York it really started moving, and I think that is what happened with black theater. As soon as it went outside of New York it really started getting over. People in those other cities don't have the alternatives that people have in New York, and so they support the cultural activities that are available.

King's optimism about the development of a nationwide black theater has been bolstered by other experiences. In 1974 he produced a touring production of Ron Milner's *What the Wine-Sellers Buy.* "We had a huge gross in Chicago," he remembers, "and only 10 percent of the audience was white." This success caused him to think that it might be possible to start a black touring program. "Cities with large black populations get black musicals," he reasoned, "but when was the last time they had anything in the way of drama?"

Over the next years, interspersed with his myriad other activities, King has pursued his idea. He has sought funding sources; contacted theater managers who might be interested in booking such an effort; he has been convincing the people who control plays that it would be worthwhile to allow touring productions of those plays; he has been talking to the "name" black actors and actresses he feels he needs in order to launch the program successfully.

If King succeeds in establishing his National Black Touring Circuit, it would be a bold step, and a risky one. The Black theater movement may have come a long way since 1960. It may be alive and vital. But there is no guarantee that the time will be right, or the support there, for a national black touring circuit. Still, as Shauneille Perry, one of King's coproducers in the venture, puts it, "The black theater movement will reflect what black people are doing. Theater is always a reflection of the times; that we know. We do not have the unity of the 1960s, but the very diffusiveness we are experiencing may be positive—it may mean that black theater is, most essentially, in the heart of black people. Black theater is here in the United States, it's in Africa, it's in Bermuda, it's in any place where black people are creating. We've got to make it where we find it. It is not handed to us. We as a people should have learned that a long time ago."

DuBois would have agreed, and so, no doubt, would Ira Aldridge and all the other talented and energetic and hopeful black people who have contributed to the history of black theater and helped to make it the challenging and creative force it is today.

Selected Bibliography

BOOKS

Cook, Mercer, and Stephen E. Henderson. *The Militant Black Writer.* Madison, Wisconsin: University of Wisconsin Press, 1969.

Dent, Thomas C., and Richard Schechner. *The Free Southern Theater by the Free Southern Theater.* Indianapolis, Indiana: The Bobbs-Merrill Company, 1969.

Fabre, Michel. *The Unfinished Quest of Richard Wright.* New York: William Morrow & Co., Inc., 1973.

Farrison, William Edward. *William Wells Brown, Author and Reformer.* Chicago, Illinois: University of Chicago Press, 1969.

Gayle, Addison, Jr. *The Black Aesthetic.* Garden City, New York: Doubleday & Co., Inc., 1972.

Green, Able, and Joe Laurie. *Show Biz.* New York: Holt & Co., 1953.

Haskins, Jim. *The Cotton Club.* New York: Random House, Inc., 1977.

Hill, Erroll. *The Theater of Black Americans.* Vols. I and II. Englewood Cliffs, New Jersey: Prentice-Hall, Inc., 1980.

Huggins, Nathan Irvin. *Harlem Renaissance.* New York: Oxford University Press, 1971.

Hughes, Langston. *The Big Sea.* New York: Alfred A. Knopf, 1945.

Hutton, Laurence. *Curiosities of the American Stage.* New York: Harper and Brothers, 1891.

Isaacs, Edith. *The Negro in the American Theatre.* New York: Theatre Arts, 1947.

174

Johnson, James Weldon. *Black Manhattan*. New York: Atheneum Publishers, 1968.

Kerlin, Robert T. *The Voice of the Negro, 1919.* New York: E. P. Dutton & Co., 1920.

Kimball, Robert, and William Bolcom. *Reminiscing with Sissle and Blake*. New York: The Viking Press, 1973.

King, Woodie, and Ron Milner. *Black Drama Anthology*. New York: Columbia University Press, 1972.

Meltzer, Milton. *Langston Hughes: A Biography*. New York: Thomas Y. Crowell Co., 1968.

Mitchell, Loften. *Black Drama: The Story of the American Negro in the Theatre*. New York: Hawthorn Books, 1967.

O'Connor, John J., and Lorraine Brown, eds. *Free, Adult, Uncensored: The Living History of the Federal Theatre Project*. Washington, D.C.: New Republic Books, 1978.

Odell, George C. D. *Annals of the New York Stage, III.* New York: Columbia University Press, 1928.

Osofsky, Gilbert. *Harlem: The Making of a Ghetto*. New York: Harper & Row, 1966.

Ottley, Roi, and William J. Weatherby, eds. *The Negro in New York: An Informal Social History*. New York: The New York Public Library, 1967.

Richardson, Ben, and William A. Fahey. *Great Black Americans,* Second Revised Edition. New York: Thomas Y. Crowell Co., 1976.

Rollins, Charlemae. *Famous Negro Entertainers of Stage, Screen & TV.* New York: Dodd, Mead & Co., 1967.

Stearns, Marshall W. *The Story of Jazz*. New York: Oxford University Press, 1958.

Sterling, Dorothy, ed. *Speak Out in Thundertones: Letters and Other Writings by Black Northerners, 1787–1865*. Garden City, New York: Doubleday & Co., Inc., 1973.

Wecter, Dixon. *The Age of the Great Depression 1929–1941.* New York: The MacMillan Co., 1948.

Wittke, Carl. *Tambo and Bones.* Durham, North Carolina: Duke University Press, 1930.

ARTICLES

Adams, George R. "Black Militant Drama." *American Image,* Vol. 28 (Summer 1971), 107–28.

Anderson, Jervis. "Dramatist," *The New Yorker,* Vol. 49 (June 16, 1973), 40ff.

Denig, Lynde. "A Unique American Playhouse." *Theatre* magazine, Vol. VI (August 1906), 32.

Haskins, Jim. "In the Theatre, Are Blacks Now Doing What They Deplored in Whites?" *Now* magazine (September 1977), 15ff.

Hay, Samuel A. "African–American Drama, 1950–1970." *Negro History Bulletin,* Vol. 36 (January 1973), 5–8.

Jefferson, Miles M. "The Negro on Broadway, 1947–48." *Phylon,* Vol. 9 (Second Quarter, 1948). Reprint.

Jones, LeRoi. "Black Drama Is the Same as Black Life." *Ebony,* Vol. 26 (February 1971), 74–76.

Moss, Robert F. "The Arts in Black America." *Saturday Review* (November 15, 1975), 12–19.

"Native Son Down Below." *New Masses* (March 10, 1942), 21.

Orton, Richard. "Black Folk Entertainments and the Evolution of American Minstrelsy." *Negro History Bulletin* (September 1978), 885–87.

"Real Coon on the American Stage." *Theatre* magazine, Vol. VI (August 1906), 44ff.

Richardson, Willis. "The Hope of a Negro Drama." *Crisis,* Vol. 19 (November 1919), 338–39.

Ross, Ronald. "The Role of Blacks in the Federal Theatre, 1935–1939." *Journal of Negro History,* Vol. 59 (January 1974), 38–50.

Toll, Robert C. "Behind the Blackface: Minstrel Men and Minstrel Myths." *American Heritage,* Vol. 29 (April 1978), 93–105.

Wallace, Michele. "For Colored Girls, the Rainbow Is Not Enough." *The Village Voice* (August 16, 1976), 104ff.

Winans, Robert B. "The Folk, the Stage, and the Five-String Banjo in the Nineteenth Century." *Journal of American Folklore,* Vol. 89 (October 1976), 407–37.

Winter, Marian Hannah. "Juba and American Minstrelsy." *Dance Index,* Vol. 6 (1947), 28–47.

OTHER SOURCES

Archives, Theatre and Music Collection, Museum of the City of New York.

Clippings files, New York Public Library for the Performing Arts, Lincoln Center.

Clippings files, New York Public Library, Schomburg Center for Research in Black Culture.

Index

Henry Street Settlement House, 125, 158, 170
Hewlett, James, 6–8, 10
Heyward, Dorothy and Dubose, 78–79, 111
Hicks, Charles, 27, 31
Hill, Abram, 114–15
Hill, J. Leubrie, 50
Hill, Ruby, 127
Hogan, Ernest, 37, 46–47
Home, 166, *167,* 168–69
Hooks, Robert, 162–63
House Committee on Un-American Activities, 106
Houseman, John, 93–94, 100, 107, 119–21
Hughes, Langston, 86–89, 114, 151, 162, 170
Hurston, Zora Neale, 86, 88
Hymn to the Rising Son, 104, 119

In Abraham's Bosom, 77–78
In Abyssinia, 42
In Dahomey, 40–42
Ingraham, Rex, 98
In White America, 141–42

Jack, Sam T., 34–35
Jeb, 136, 138
Jelliffe, Russell and Rowena, 88
Johnson, J. Rosamond, 37, 46, 49, 56, 113
Johnson, Hall, 101
Jolson, Al, 31
Jones, James Earl, 152
Jones, LeRoi. *See* Baraka, Imamu Amiri
Jones, Sissieretta, 35–36
Joplin, Scott, 52
"Juba," 23–25

Karamu House, 82, 88–89, 169–70
Kean, Edmund, 11

Keith theater circuit, 62, 64
Kersands, Billy, 27, *29,* 30, 33
King Lear, 12–13
King, Woodie, Jr., 158, 170–72
Korean War, 128–29
Krigwa Players, the, 70–71, 82, 156

Lafayette Theatre, 49–52, 78, 82, 94, 98–100, 127, 149
 stock company, 47, 49–51, 56, 58, 64
Last Breeze of Summer, The, 165
Lee, Canada, 95, 113, 117, 121, *122,* 123, 136
Lincoln Theatre, 52, 89
 stock company, 47, 52–53, 58, 64
little theater, 70, 86–87, 124
Los Angeles, California, black theater in, 100–102, 114
Lucas, Sam, 28, 34–35
Lyles, Aubrey, 50, 63–64, 66, 124
Lysistrata, 102

Macbeth, 12–13, 95–96, 100, 123
Macbeth, Robert, 149
Mamba's Daughters, 110, *111,* 112
Mayfield, Julian, 138
McClendon, Rose, 77, *79,* 86, 90–94
McClendon, Rose, Players, 115, 136
McClintic, Guthrie, 111
Medal for Willie, A, 128–29
Member of the Wedding, The, 113
Miller, Flournoy, 50, 63–64, 66, 124, 127
Milner, Ron, 170, 177
Mitchell, Abbie, 77–78
Mitchell, Lofton, 131

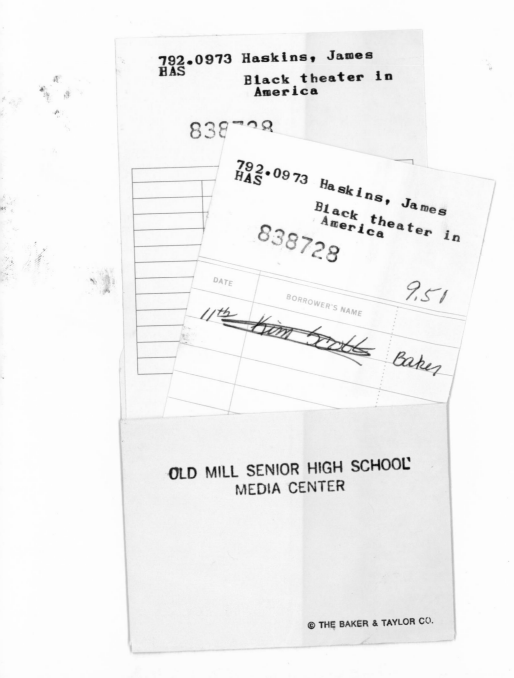

792.0973 Haskins, James
HAS
Black theater in
America

838728

792.0973 Haskins, James
HAS
Black theater in
America

838728

9.51

DATE	BORROWER'S NAME	
11th	~~Kim Scott~~	Baker

OLD MILL SENIOR HIGH SCHOOL
MEDIA CENTER